The Beginner's Guide to Investing in Real Estate:

How Small Investors Can Achieve Wealth and Financial Freedom for Life

Jeffry Stevens

© Copyright 2020 - All rights reserved.

The content contained within this book may not be reproduced, duplicated or transmitted without direct written permission from the author or the publisher.

Under no circumstances will any blame or legal responsibility be held against the publisher, or author, for any damages, reparation, or monetary loss due to the information contained within this book, either directly or indirectly.

Legal Notice:

This book is copyright protected. It is only for personal use. You cannot amend, distribute, sell, use, quote or paraphrase any part, or the content within this book, without the consent of the author or publisher.

Disclaimer Notice:

Please note the information contained within this document is for educational and entertainment purposes only. All effort has been executed to present accurate, up to date, reliable, complete information. No warranties of any kind are declared or implied. Readers acknowledge that the author is not engaged in the rendering of legal, financial, medical or professional advice. The content within this book has been derived from various sources. Please consult a licensed professional before attempting any techniques outlined in this book.

By reading this document, the reader agrees that under no circumstances is the author responsible for any losses, direct or indirect, that are incurred as a result of the use of the information contained within this document, including, but not limited to, errors, omissions, or inaccuracies.

Table of Contents

Introduction 6
Chapter 1: Where Are You? 19
    Stage One: Holding On 22
    Stage Two: Stability 25
    Stage Three: Dragon 28
    Stage Four: Flourish 30
    Stage Five: Profit 32
    Stage Six: Financial Freedom 32
    Determination 33
Chapter 2: Get Out 35
    Stage Three: Dragon 36
    Stage One and Two: Holding on and Stability 40
    Stage Four: Flourish 44
    Stage Five: Profit 46
    Stage Six: Financial Freedom 47
Chapter 3: This Little Piggy Knows Which Market 49
    Local 52
    Near-ish 54
    Big Picture 55
    Small Picture 56
    Benefits 59
Chapter 4: Write It Up 62
    Target Property 63

Property Niche 64
Seller Niche 65
End-User Niche 65

Write It Down 66

Chapter 5: There's No 'I' in Team 69

VIP Circle 71

Sub-Circle 74

Growth Team 75

Chapter 6: Financing 79

Financing Options 82
Portfolio Loans 82
FHA 83
203k Loans 83
Owner Financing 83
Hard Money Loans 84
Private Money 85
Home Equity 85
Commercial Loans 86

Let's Talk About Cash 87
Save 89
Sell 90
Borrow 91
Partner 92

Chapter 7: Passive Income 93

Active Income 94

Passive Income 96

Property Management 98

Chapter 8: Property Know-How 103

Mortgage 104

Down Payment 105

Rental Income 105

Price to Income Ratio 106
Price-to-Rent Ratio 107
Gross Rental Yield 108
Capitalization Rate 108
Cash Flow 109
Other Important Things to Consider 110
   Utilities 110
   HOA 111
   Property Management 111
   Maintenance 112
   Vacancy 113
   Other Expenses 114

Chapter 9: Wealth and Financial Freedom 116

Cash Flow 119
Appreciation 120
Depreciation 120
Loans 122
Leverage 123
Forced Equity 123
Inflation 125

Chapter 10: Next Steps 127

Schedule 130
Prioritize 135

Conclusion 140

References 146

INTRODUCTION

You are sipping your favorite cocktail while digging your toes into warm white sand. If you look to your left and right, that white sand stretches beyond the horizon. There's a tropical breeze running across your skin keeping you cool as the sun rises higher and higher in the sky. At the same time, the brilliant blue ocean, see-through like glass, laps gently on the beach providing a perfect soundtrack to your day. You feel happy and full, like you could stay here forever.

You can't believe you are here, in paradise. The place so many people dream about. All of your hard work finally paid off and you get to sit back and enjoy life. Right now, the only thing on your mind is what murder mystery paperback you should read next. The only thing scheduled for today is to reapply sunscreen in 30 minutes. Life can be a dream, can't it?

Only, it is a dream. Your 6 a.m. alarm jerks you from the white sand beach, the cocktail disappears from your hand, and reality sinks back in. The only white that stretches here is your duvet stretching to the end of the bed. That old duvet with that wine spill that you could never get out, glaring up at you.

You roll over, reaching out to hit snooze on your blaring alarm. You roll back over, squeezing your eyes tight, desperately trying to transport yourself back to paradise. You try to chant, "There is no place like the beach, there is no place like the beach, there is no place like the beach."

It doesn't work. Five minutes later the snooze expires and you are awake. You are fully awake and staring at your peppercorn ceiling that you hate and keep meaning to change. You have things that you have to do, responsibilities that you have to take care of. Reluctantly, you pull off the covers and get out of bed.

Your feet move sluggishly across your bedroom floor as you walk into the kitchen to start the coffee maker. As you try to shake the hazy sleep out of your body, you look around you and realize for the first time how dimly lit your house is. Maybe it only seems this way because half of your mind is still in your dream, on the beach as the warm sun beats down on the white sand and makes the water sparkle.

It is Monday morning. Your day starts just like any other day. This same thing happened last week and the week before that. It is like a never-ending cycle. As you brush your teeth and look at your reflection in your bathroom mirror, you wonder if there is a way to break out of this routine. For now, you slug on like the rest of the world, going through the motions. Living from month to month, paycheck to paycheck. Overall, this life strategy works. At least, it has worked so far. It is functional and what you honestly expected to be doing by this point in life. You work a regular 9-5 job. You have a regular income that covers your living expenses. Most people would describe your life as ideal, something to be grateful for.

And you do appreciate it. At the end of the day, you recognize and appreciate that you do have a stable job and income. There are people out there in worse situations than you right now who wish they could be standing in your kitchen. You are relatively content with your life. But why does it still feel off? If this is the life that you always pictured, then why are you not fully satisfied?

As you toast your morning bagel and sip your fresh cup of coffee, that feeling from before creeps back into your mind. What if there is a way to pay off those student loans faster or those credit card bills? What if you could find a way to pay off your car and house, or even upgrade to a bigger place? Or maybe there is a business idea that you have always wanted to pursue, but it has always been too risky. As you allow yourself to start to think of the future possibilities, your ideas start to snowball. One builds on top of the other until you are imagining yourself back at the beach from your dream, relaxing in paradise. You force yourself to come back to reality, back to your kitchen. Your dreams can wait, because for now, it is time to go to work. It is time to face your day. You do not want to be late.

When you really let yourself think of the future, there are so many possible outcomes open to you. Take a moment to think through a few dream scenarios. Everyone has at least one far-fetched dream that they think about now and again. You probably have one too, that little dream that you think about to escape from reality for just a few moments. Take a moment now to conjure up your best dream, no matter how far out of reach it may seem.

Now, how do you get started toward that dream, and where do you look to begin?

Congrats to you for picking up this book! Maybe you have a colleague who started investing in real estate, or you read a great article about the benefits and opportunities of pursuing a passive income. Whatever brought you to this book, we are glad that you are here. Together, we are going to learn about what it takes to start investing in real estate.

Throughout these next 10 chapters, we are going to work together to help you understand the options available to you in regard to real estate investing, generating passive income, and ultimately how to achieve financial freedom. If you do not know what some of these are, do not fear, we have the answers for you in the following sections. By opening this book, you've just unlocked your future.

Life achievement +1, proceed to the next tile.

In these next 10 chapters, we will go over everything that you need to know to start investing in real estate. There is a lot of information packed into each chapter. We encourage you to keep a pen and notebook handy to write down ideas as they come to you or questions that might pop up as you read. If you prefer a more digital approach, grab your laptop, tablet, or phone as an alternative. The format of your notes does not matter. This is a great way to keep track of your thoughts that you can sift through later. In a few instances, we will prompt you with questions to get you thinking about where you are, what you want to accomplish, etc. Jotting down notes will help you keep track of your ideas and plans.

Before we jump in and dig our heels into the exciting world of real estate investing, flip back to the table of contents. Browse through the subjects that we are going to focus on in the subsequent chapters. We have designed each chapter to build on top of the previous ones to create a flow of information that is easy for you to follow. It is recommended that you follow in order to get the most out of it. Feel free to flip back to chapters for a refresher as you go along, but try not to skip too far ahead, you might miss something important by skipping around.

Another thing to note, for simplicity's sake and to make sure we are all on the same page, we are going to approach every topic from an absolute beginner's point of view. Maybe you already have a base understanding of some of the terms or ideas that we address in this book. Maybe you majored in business or finance in college or took some classes, read some books, or attended some seminars already. That's great! Give yourself a pat on the back for having a leg up on everyone else. Now put your hand back down, we don't want to get too cocky here. Even if you think you know some things already, we are going to assume that you don't. And hey, you might just learn something new if you keep an open mind.

Now, let us introduce you to the main character of our book, Jerry Investment. Every book needs a protagonist, right? Throughout these next chapters, we are going to follow Jerry along in his path toward financial freedom. By using this fictional character, we hope that it will make complicated ideas seem realistic and doable. We also hope that you will be able to visualize your potential journey in real estate investing. Right now, Jerry is like our underdog. He never imagined that he would be investing in real estate, but after hearing some stories, he thinks that this investment path might just be what he is looking for. Let's be Jerry's cheerleaders together! He's going to need it to get through this next stage in life.

Jerry is getting by in life. He has enough of an income to get by month to month with a little cushion for extra expenses, fun events, or emergencies. Jerry is not a big saver right now. This is primarily because he has a few student loans to finish paying, a small car payment, and he bought a small starter home about 2 years ago. You could say that Jerry is doing o.k., but he is beginning to wonder if there is more opportunity for growth in his savings.

Maybe Jerry's situation sounds familiar to you. Maybe it is the exact situation that you are in right now. Don't worry, we are not psychic, this is just a very average situation that people find themselves in. Even if it is not your exact situation, we hope that you find some connection to Jerry's journey that you can apply to your own.

The hard truth is, real estate investing is not a quick and easy way to make bank. If that is what you are thinking right now, sit down and take note, real estate investing takes time, a little bit of money, and a few vials of sweat. You are going to have to put in some work, but the reward makes up for everything.

We do not want to start you off with the wrong ideas, and we do not intend to sugarcoat anything about this process. That will not do you any favors in the long run. Yes, what you have probably heard is true. Investing in real estate is one of the most sought after and smartest ways to generate wealth in this modern age. That is for a couple of reasons that we will get into later. To give you an idea at the start, real estate is relatively stable (compared to other investment strategies) and you do not need to be rich to get into it. Yes! You read that correctly. You do not need to be rich to get started investing in real estate. How can that be? Keep reading to find out.

Although real estate investments are a great and functional way to generate wealth, you need to understand that there is a risk to it. Even if you do everything right, follow all of the best advice, there is still a chance that you might not succeed or that you might lose your investment. We do not mean to be negative here, just realistic. If you go into real estate investing with this in mind, you will not be surprised or taken off guard when (or if) it happens. This means that you can be smart about your choices and build up a defense against potential losses. So if you get into a pickle, you can get right back out.

Do not be worried, just be realistic. In this book, we are going to give you tips and tools to learn about the business. You can then use this knowledge to fuel other research and make smart and safe decisions. Think of this book as your armor. We are here to help you succeed in the way that is best for you. We hope that you learn a lot, and we hope that you will enjoy the learning process.

If you are reading this book, we are assuming that you think investing in real estate is a good way to generate income. You are not wrong. You have probably heard stories of multi-millionaires who got their start in real estate. It is true that a lot of successful millionaires got their start in real estate investing as well. If you have heard their success stories, then you have probably also heard some of their failures.

As we mentioned, investing in real estate is not a quick and easy way to make a buck, it is also not guaranteed. Although the tips and tricks in this book are good tips and a good foundation of knowledge that you can use to your benefit, there are a lot of fluctuations in this market that can affect whether or not you succeed. Some of these fluctuations you can protect yourself from, others you have no control over. That is just a fact of the business. However, failure is not the end in this business, sometimes it is just the beginning. If something goes wrong, pick yourself up, dust yourself off, and get back to it. If you approach your losses or stumbles as learning opportunities, then you have the right attitude.

Now, take a few minutes to close your eyes and imagine your goal. It does not have to be the far-fetched dream that you conjured up earlier. You can start with something more realistic if you choose. Or you can sit back and visualize the best and craziest future that you want for yourself or for your family. Do it right now, just close your eyes and let yourself dream. We will wait while you do, just do not take too long, we have a lot yet to learn.

Back already? How did your future look? Take out that piece of paper and pen that you are supposed to have next to you and scribble down a bullet point list of your future goals. Start with the small goals that you might have, like paying off a loan, then slowly progress to bigger goals, like retiring by age 45. You do not have to be too specific right now and do not worry, you can always adjust your goals as you go. When you are done, box it off so we can keep those goals separate and flip back to them whenever you need a little boost of inspiration or if you need to adjust them at all.

The scenario that we opened with, cocktails on a white sand beach, that is Jerry's goal. Jerry wants to find a way to expand his savings, pay off his debts, and retire on a beach in the Caribbean by 45.

In reality, most people get involved in the business of real estate investing because they want to retire early. With the younger generations reaching adulthood, they have fostered the idea of removing the typical retirement age. Rightfully so. As you have probably heard in the news in the past decade, social security benefits will not be available to the younger generations by the time they reach 65, or retirement. This started out as a frustrating problem, but it encouraged people to get creative with their savings.

We have ushered in the age of the side hustle. More than ever, most people work more than one job. This looks different for everyone, but the idea of a side hustle (or making an extra income to cushion your savings) is very appealing and can be lucrative.

Side hustles are helped along the way by our digital age. Now, you do not have to physically go to a second job at a certain time of day. Now, you can pick up a remote side hustle. This works for most people because they can work their side hustles around their families, hobbies, and main job. The freedom to work whenever and wherever you can is very appealing, but in most cases, side hustles do not generate a lot of wealth nor do they generate a passive income. That is why people turn to real estate.

Real estate is unique in many ways, as most you will discover for yourself along your journey. We will highlight a few now to give you a good idea. As we mentioned before, you do not need to be rich to get involved in real estate (we will talk about what money you do need later). Real estate investing is also unique because you do not need to have a formal degree in business or finance. Any adult at any educational level can get involved in real estate investing. If you do a quick internet search, you can find stories of how broke college students took control of their finances and got involved in real estate investing. It really is fascinating to hear these success stories!

When you start to invest your time in real estate, a whole host of opportunities open up to you. If you can dream it, you can visualize it and make an actionable plan to achieve your goal.

Maybe you prefer a mountain chalet over the Caribbean or you want to be financially free to travel full-time. These are all perfect ideas and we are so proud of you for dreaming big. In these next 10 chapters, we are going to give you the knowledge and the tools to do these things. We are going to introduce you to the terms of real estate investing.

We are going to help you understand how and where to get started. We are going to discuss the ideas of passive income and financial freedom. But most importantly, we are going to have a little fun while we do it!

Now, let's make those dreams reality and start you on your path to financial freedom.

Chapter 1: Where Are You?

Hello, welcome to the first chapter of this book and welcome to the rest of your life. We are so glad that you made it here in this time and space, and we are excited to go through this process with you.

We may be coming from different places at different times, but we all have the same goal in mind. We have heard that investing in real estate is a great way to generate wealth and passive income. As we talked about in the introduction, this is an appealing idea to most of us here in the modern age. The great news is that now is the best and easiest time to get involved in real estate investing. As we dive into the different chapters, we will see just how simple it really can be.

Okay, so you want to get started in real estate investing. Great! But where do you start? How much money do you need to start? What if your current financial state is not great? Do you need degrees or licensing to invest? Should you take a seminar or classes to learn about the market? Should you do this alone or with a partner? Will you have to manage your properties yourself?

There are probably so many questions circling through your head right now. Take a moment and take a deep breath, let's try to clear your headspace before we begin.

If you are a little confused in the beginning, do not worry, you are not alone. If you are asking yourself any of the above questions right now, rest assured, they will all be answered in due time.

Real estate investing can seem a little intimidating at first glance. You might have some preconceived notions based on stories or news that you have heard in the past. Just in the past decade, the overall real estate market has seen significant fluctuations that may be at the back of your mind as we dive into our book.

Before we begin, we encourage you to take those preconceived notions and throw them out the window. Let us start from a clean slate; let us pretend that we know nothing about real estate or investing. As we talked about in the introduction, we are going to go over easy, beginner-friendly steps that will lead you toward your goal. Approaching these investment strategies from a fresh mindset is the best way to get started.

The good news is that the very first step toward investing in real estate is very easy! In this first chapter, we are going to take a deep dive into your current financial state. That is it!

To start, you have to know where you are. Sounds pretty simple and straightforward, right? However, it is critical that you be honest with yourself at this point. Be honest about your current situation and be realistic about changes that you can make to improve your finances. Lying to yourself now will only increase your struggles later.

We made this first chapter very easy for you to get started and toss your worries out the door. All you have to do is take a look at your finances and determine which financial stage below best matches your present financial situation. No decisions are going to be made in this chapter, we will save that for later sections. In Chapter 2, we will then build on the information from this chapter to find ways for you to move on from your current financial state.

Let's start by conjuring up our main character, Jerry Investment. You remember Jerry, right? Jerry has a goal to expand his savings, pay off his debts, and retire on a beach in the Caribbean.

The very first thing that Jerry has to do is to figure out where he stands financially. Now, Jerry is a very visual kind of guy so we are going to build a little picture for him to understand the levels of finances.

As we mentioned in the introduction, Jerry has a small starter home. Let's say that he has a formal living room in this house that he has yet to decorate. It's a clean, open room with a large picture window in the front that lets in a lot of light. Jerry does not know what he can do with this room right now, but he's hoping to build up the room to a fully furnished decorator's dream.

As we develop this scenario, remember that this is a simple metaphor for real estate investing. See if there are any parallels that you can discern from the story that we create. Let's dive in.

STAGE ONE: HOLDING ON

So Jerry is standing in the middle of this empty room, thinking through his finances, and realizes that he does not have any extra cash to add furniture to the room.

He has an idea! Jerry has an old futon from his college days that's stored in his parents' basement.

The first thing Jerry does is run over to his parents' house to pick up this futon. He thinks this is a great starting place; furniture he already owns! When he removes the old floral sheet that's keeping the dust off of the old futon he sees what state the futon is in. Let's just say, this futon has seen one too many parties. But at least it is something, Jerry says to himself. He loads the futon into the back of his car.

As he is leaving, his parents stop him and say, "Hey, we have a couch from your great aunt's house in the garage that she gave us when she sold her home. Why don't you take it? It's just gathering dust in the garage, at least you can put it to some use."

Now Jerry is really excited. Even if the futon is a little worse for wear, now he has a fully functional couch!

Jerry agrees to take the couch off of his parents' hands, and they say they will drop it off later today. Perfect, Jerry is already on his way to making a fully functional front room.

Only, Jerry forgot how his great aunt used to style her home. When his parents pull into his driveway and place the couch in his front room, he gets a little nervous. Flashbacks of lace doilies, overstuffed china cabinets, mismatched floral wallpaper that makes you dizzy, and caramel candies flood Jerry's memory. Now he has a decomposing futon under the picture window and a plastic-covered brown floral couch against the far wall.

Needless to say, this is not what Jerry pictured for his front room, but it is all that he has right now, so it will have to do.

Right now, Jerry is just holding on. You could say that he is living paycheck to paycheck. He has just enough to pay the bills that need to be paid, but there isn't any wiggle room in his budget. In this visual scene, Jerry is living on borrowed or worn-out furniture.

Now, Jerry could easily keep on going this way. He has managed to get through this far, why not keep going?

But a small voice in the back of his mind keeps nagging him. What if a pipe bursts in the house, what if I get into a car accident next week and have to repair or replace my car? What if?

That's where Jerry is right now, in a state of what-ifs. So many things could go wrong, and he is realizing that he does not have enough cash on hand to take care of things if they do.

As Jerry looks at the plain and mismatched state of his front room, he decides that he could make some decisions to increase his monthly income.

Maybe you are at this financial stage. You know that you have enough to get by or maybe you have some debts; whether they are student loans or credit card bills, there's probably something holding you back from growing financially.

If this is you, take out your pen and paper and write down all of your monthly and yearly expenses. Take stock of your normal bills, like rent and utilities, car or homeowners insurance. Then jot down any debts you owe, how much you started with, and how much you still need to pay. Finally, write down any extra expenses that occur. Make sure you write everything down, haircuts, groceries, phone bill, take-out, coffee runs, you get it.

Do you notice any patterns in the extra expenses? Jot down some patterns if you notice them. We will come back to them in the next chapter.

STAGE TWO: STABILITY

In stage two, Jerry has the same front room with his great aunt's couch and his decomposing futon from college.

In this stage of stability, Jerry has some extra cash left over every month. Just enough to add some cosmetic improvements to the room.

After looking over his monthly spending, Jerry picks up a can of paint at the home improvement store. He moves the furniture away from the walls and slaps on a fresh coat of paint. The room is now significantly brighter, but Jerry does not have enough money to keep going this month.

When the next month comes around, Jerry picks up a used rug in pristine condition from a vintage store in town. While he is at the vintage store, he sees a coffee table that he really likes. Since there is no room in his budget this time, he decides to pass on it and come back for it next month. He places the rug in the room.

Entering the third month of improvements, Jerry rushes over to the vintage store and finds the coffee table waiting for him! He loads it into the car. On his way home, Jerry stops by his local box store to pick up two dust covers for the couch and futon.

He goes home and adds these minor improvements to his room. He thinks this isn't too bad.

Month by month, Jerry keeps adding small improvements. It takes a really long time, especially later when he wants to replace the futon and couch with newer and nicer pieces. Jerry has to save for months or choose to take out financing to afford these new changes.

In this stage, Jerry has enough money left over each month to add incremental changes to his room. He is living even more comfortably than before but as we saw, if he bought everything that he wanted to buy all at once, he would have to put it on a credit card and make monthly payments toward it. Although this is doable, it is not the solution that Jerry wants to get the room of his dreams.

Again, Jerry could easily keep on living like this; at least now he is not embarrassed by the state of his front room.

If you look at your monthly budget and see a similar situation, you are probably in the stability stage. Maybe you use the extra cash every month to treat yourself or maybe you save it for a rainy day or unexpected costs (medical bills, accidents, etc.). A lot of people probably see themselves in this stage, and most never truly get out of it. It is comfy in this stage, may we even say, stable?

Now you have to ask yourself, if you stayed in this stage, could you achieve your goal of financial freedom?

Let's keep going.

STAGE THREE: DRAGON

Now Jerry has a fully functional front room that is comfortable enough that people can come over for dinner parties. Yet, Jerry knows that this room could be better.

Jerry sits down at the covered floral couch and makes a list of everything he wants to do to the room to make it even better.

- Change the overhead lighting
- Replace the futon with extra seating
- Add more lighting with lamps
- Add side tables
- Build a bookcase
- Find some books to add to the bookcase
- Get some plants
- Add accent pieces to tables

Needless to say, Jerry has a lot of ideas. At this stage, he has the extra money to do it all. He even decides to build his own bookcase and side tables.

Off he goes to the home improvement store to pick up all of the supplies he needs and gets building.

After he buys, builds, and places everything, he hosts a fun dinner party with a few close friends. Everyone marvels at the room, in particular the bookcase and side tables that Jerry made. This makes Jerry very happy and he finds himself wanting to keep adding to his room. More and more until it is stuffed to the brim. Jerry now turns into a dragon.

Okay, we had a little fun with this stage. Chances are, you are not a dragon, neither is Jerry. We chose this title because when you think of a dragon, you might think of its hoards of gold and jewels. Jerry had more than enough resources to really dig in and build the room of his dreams.

As we saw in this third stage, Jerry was able to replace furniture and pick up a lot of little extra pieces to add to his front room. The room is now full of things and ready to welcome guests! That was the goal, right? Still, Jerry comes up with an idea...

STAGE FOUR: FLOURISH

Jerry has a fully furnished and functioning room, but he is still not satisfied. He knows now that he can keep adding. However, this time, he is not going to add to his front room.

Jerry calls a friend. His friend answers and raves about Jerry's dinner party. Jerry says, "That's why I am calling you. I have an idea."

"Go on..."

"I want to start a furniture business, and I want you to be my business partner."

"A furniture business? But how would we start?"

"I have the building plans for my side tables and bookcases, we start there. I'll build, and you get the clients. We will have to start small, building for friends and family. That will get the word out about our business. Then, once we get a good footing, we add more products. Maybe we start a website or a flagship store. That we can decide later. For now, we start small and see where it gets us. What do you say?"

"Let's do it. I'll be our first client."

Jerry started out with an idea to decorate his front room, and now he has a business idea. It may be small right now, but with time and dedication, it could very well flourish.

When you are in this fourth stage, you go beyond what you have, build on your resources, and start to make some moves. They will not be big at first. Jerry and his friend are going to need to put in a lot of time and sweat to make this happen. At first, they will only make enough to cover their expenses. As word gets out and they begin to grow, they will add extra cash that they can then put back into their business, and on the cycle goes.

Do you see the parallel to real estate investing? Jerry and his friend have an idea, they are going to write up a business plan, and get out there. This stage is just the beginning.

STAGE FIVE: PROFIT

At this financial stage, you already have some personal equity that you can then use to grow more investment opportunities. This stage is less about savings and more about making money with existing assets. How can you turn $1 into $10?

In our furniture-driven scenario, Jerry and his friend have started to turn a small profit in their furniture business. Now they are looking to build upon this success. To do this, they know that they need more clients and they need to upgrade their working space.

Jerry and his friend begin to search out and research a larger workshop with a storefront where they can put their furniture models on display.

STAGE SIX: FINANCIAL FREEDOM

Jerry and his friend have built a business. Over the past 15 years, they have flourished and saved. Now, they are deciding that they want to step away from an active role in the business. They have an option to sell the business for a profit to a competitor or pass the management of the business on to someone else.

In both of these scenarios, Jerry and his friend are looking to take a less active role in their business. Jerry has had his beach goal in the back of his mind throughout the years, and now he sees that his dream can be a reality.

If you place yourself in this stage and say, "Hey I'm already there," then why are you reading this book?

All in good jest, if you are reading this book, then this stage is probably your end goal. This is the financial stage where your living expenses (and beyond) are covered by the income generated by your investments. We won't dwell on this stage for too long, because other chapters will dive into the idea further.

DETERMINATION

Chances are, if you are reading this book, you might fall into one of the first three stages. Never fear! In the following chapters, we are going to take a deep dive into how you can look beyond your present state and progress to your future goal of financial freedom. Keep reading to find out just how to do that.

We hope that the furniture-driven scenario boils down the larger and complex idea of real estate into a simpler idea. When you look closer, you can see the parallels between the two.

Do you know which stage you are currently in? It does not have to fit your life perfectly; this experiment is intended to give you a better idea of where you are, in order for us to build upon your financial stage. That is the end goal, isn't it? To find a way to generate wealth through a passive income and achieve financial freedom.

Before we continue on, take out that scrap of paper and draw a straight or slanted vertical line. At the bottom add the label holding on. As you draw up the line, keep adding the different stages that we just reviewed all the way up to the top or end of the line. If you are in a good mood, draw a little person next to whichever stage you are in. Any little stick figure will do, no need for dramatic drawings here.

Now, bring your little figure to the next chapter, and let's review how you can move this little guy up the line.

Chapter 2: Get Out

I n this chapter, we are going to go through some examples of ways that you can increase your savings, start to pay off debts, and learn about the field at the same time. We encourage you to check out the examples for all of the stages and make notes of ideas that intrigue you. You might be in financial stage four, but like an idea listed in stage one and two and so on. Keep an open mind and let's explore your options.

What is great about this section is that you can get started on these ideas before you even know what areas of the real estate market that you want to invest in. Most of the early strategies listed below are separate from the real estate market or they help you get to know the field before investing your own time and money into a property.

Now, let us explore some options to help you move up the stairs and improve your financial situation.

STAGE THREE: DRAGON

To get to stage three, you are going to need to start to get creative with your resources and living situation. The goal in this scenario is to dramatically add to your savings at a faster rate than before. This is done by either reducing expenses or increasing your income.

Any of the above strategies will work to help you achieve this goal, which is great if you are already doing that! Good for you for getting a head start.

A lot of the ideas in the first two stages are ways that you can cut costs. When you are looking to dramatically expand your savings, these are important cuts to keep doing. Going back on them now will only slow you down or force you backward. Obviously, this is not something you want to do. If you can control it, you should only be moving forward at this point. Of course, there are things out of your control that might have some effect on this forward movement. If that happens, try not to get bent out of shape by it. Accept it and restart.

So what can you do?

You can hack your housing. Be careful with this idea, because in some places there are laws against certain "hacks". Make sure you know the rules before you do something. This will save you from having to deal with any legal issues, which will also save you money. There are a lot of ways to hack your housing. Do some quick internet searches to find some ideas. Again, we want to stress that you do your research and make sure that you know what you are getting into. A fun and modern way to hack your housing is to use services like Airbnb. Do you have an extra room that you can open up to short-term rentals? Or maybe you have a pool house that you can convert; there are a lot of different options. People get really creative with this idea, and that creativity pays off because renters like to stay in unique places.

Another option is to do a live-in flip. You can do this to gain experience and build on your real estate knowledge. A live-in flip is just as it sounds, you live in a house while you repair it. In this scenario, you have to be okay with some extra dust or paint fumes, and you have to keep your possessions small and organized in order to move around a bit. Do some research on this idea, because there are some tax savings available to you.

In a similar fashion, you can downsize your house. If you already have a house, you can sell it and purchase a much smaller property. You can then live in this house for a few years, then keep it to use as a rental later on. Not only will you be adding to the value with cosmetic changes, the longer you have the property, the more value it will generate over time. We will talk about value growth much later in the book.

We mentioned this next idea in the first section, but it is so good that we want to mention it again. That is, start a non-real estate side hustle. When we first talked about this idea, we asked you to do some quick searches to get a good idea of what is available to you. Go ahead and pick two of those side hustles, and do some more research on them. Start to seek out open opportunities to prepare. These side hustles, you can do at any time in your process. It is just a good idea to get started when the opportunity is available to you.

STAGE ONE AND TWO: HOLDING ON AND STABILITY

We combined these two stages because they are pretty similar and the strategies to improve your situation for these two stages are the same. As we mentioned before, keep an open mind about these strategies, because many of them are great ways to build your knowledge of the industry and add to your savings which you can then put toward your future investments.

If you are in one of these two financial stages, then you have enough to get by, but your immediate goal is to increase your monthly income and savings for future investment opportunities and avoid any losses along the way.

How do you do that?

In the last chapter, we asked you to take a look at your monthly budget and see if you noticed any patterns. Pull out those notes right now and review them. Do you tend to spend a lot of money on take-out for lunches and dinner? Do you spend too much on coffee runs? A great place to start is to seek out little expenses like this that you can cut or replace from your budget. For example, instead of ordering take-out for lunch, pack your own lunch. Even if you live around the corner from a great coffee shop, start skipping your daily coffee runs and opt to make your own coffee instead. If you truly cannot part with the coffee from the coffee shop, see if they offer any bagged grounds that you can buy and take home. This is a smart way to take something you love and replace it with something that will ultimately save you money. At the same time, by finding a creative alternative like this, you are not actually giving up on something that you love, just saving money. You have probably heard these tips before. They are a perfect beginning point to pack your monthly budget a little. Set these savings aside.

Another quick and easy thing to do is to keep your day job and work toward a raise. Learn how to negotiate for a higher salary. If you work hourly, take on some extra hours. Again, these first two don't deal with real estate, but the extra savings that you can accrue with these two strategies will help you out in the long run.

Dip your toe into the business by becoming a buyer's agent. As a buyer's agent, you will help buyers find the perfect property, negotiate offers for buyers, help buyers find other real estate professionals (like attorneys, inspectors, contractors, etc.), and advise buyers on issues that may arise during the process. Becoming a buyer's agent is a great way to break into the real estate business. This position will introduce you to the real estate process and help you build a network of professionals that you can keep for later use. We will discuss the dynamics of building teams in Chapter 5.

Similarly, you can become a leasing agent. As a leasing agent, you will work for a property owner by managing the property for them. You will seek out tenants for the property and handle the business side of property management (like signing leases, evaluating properties, and acting as a landlord on the property). Like buyer's agents, becoming a leasing agent will help you learn the ropes of the real estate business by handling things for another owner, without the personal risk. This is a fantastic way to get hands-on experience in the real estate industry.

Team up with a team of house flippers or a rehabilitation team and manage their projects. This is a great way to network and meet fellow investors. It's also a great way to see the remodeling process from an outsider's perspective for future prospects.

Work on a side hustle that is based on a passion of yours to generate an additional source of income.

This side hustle could be related to real estate, like landscaping, decorating, furniture building, or design, etc. Or it could be an unrelated passion that will help you expand your savings to pay off your debts or set money aside to put toward future investment opportunities. In this digital age, the number of side hustles that are available to you is endless. To get a good idea of what is available, go ahead and do a quick web search for side hustles. Right now! You will find a whole host of articles, lists, and videos related to this subject. For most of these side hustles, you can now work remotely, and for most, you can create your own schedule. That gives you the flexibility to work as many or as few extra hours as you can put aside each week. During your web search, jot down a few ideas that speak to you right now. This is a great way to just get thinking about your options.

In our fictional scenario, our main character, Jerry, wants to focus on learning as much of the business as possible before he jumps in with his first investment. Jerry is considering all of his options and makes a pros and cons list for each avenue of extra income. He decides that he wants to get his hand dirty and help out on a team of house flippers. He just happens to know a friend from his college days that is a full-time flipper, two towns over.

Jerry reaches out to show his interest and soon he is tearing down walls and making connections!

All of these options are a great way to get your foot in the door, increase your income, and learn different aspects of the real estate business without stepping into the risk just yet.

STAGE FOUR: FLOURISH

In this next stage, you are going to take all of the ideas and strategies that you have already started and keep building on those plans. The goal for this next stage is to grow your smaller savings into much larger savings. That sounds kind of vague, doesn't it?

All of the strategies in the first two sections are only going to generate a certain amount of extra income or extra savings. To really grow, you are going to need to put in place some big and actionable strategies to truly create positive savings.

A fun idea is to start flipping houses. This is not the same as the last flip where you live in the property. This is an accelerated version of the flipping process. If you've worked on a team of flippers in the past (like in section one) you can then use the knowledge and network connections that you created to build your own team. This is a great way to turn a quick profit that you can save or use to reinvest in other properties. Do lots of research and find the best strategy that works for you. Be wary of money pits and make smart decisions.

Another way to significantly grow your savings is to build or grow a property portfolio. There are a few different strategies that you can use to achieve this. We will list a few, but we encourage you to do your own research and find some other options that are available to you.

- Pay for properties using all-cash offers. This strategy means that you will not be collecting any additional debts.
- Get financing to buy a small group of properties, then use any cash flow from those properties to pay off your debt quickly, one property at a time. Think of rentals for this idea.
- A popular idea is to buy three different rental properties of equal (or at least similar commodities and price), hold them for a little bit, then sell two of them. The profits that you make from selling the two properties can then be put into the third property that you chose to keep. This helps you accelerate your payments and move to own the property faster.

STAGE FIVE: PROFIT

As we saw before, each stage grows from the last to help you keep moving forward. We are going to keep going with our last stage.

In this stage, the overall goal is to maximize your property value to increase your income. This can be done in a few different ways.

The first and most logical idea is to sell low-quality properties and buy higher quality properties that are going to make you more money or mature better. For example, if you used the strategy to buy three rentals, sell two, and keep one, it might be time to sell the rental that you kept and invest in a better piece of property. We will talk about cash-flow and evaluating properties later.

You can also refinance any debts that you may have with better fixed-rate options. This will save you money in the long run.

If you do not have any properties under your name at the moment, you can invest in properties that will generate passive income for you like residential rentals or investing in a partnership where you do not have to do the maintenance work.

When you get to this stage, chances are that you will have a pretty good working knowledge of the industry. By this point, you have probably worked in the industry for a few years, and gone through a few different property strategies. You can then use this knowledge to invest in other investors. If someone comes to you and wants to get started in real estate (just like you are right now!) hear out their plan and invest in it if you think they have what it takes. Keep in mind where you started, and give someone else the opportunity to start as well.

STAGE SIX: FINANCIAL FREEDOM

Financial freedom. That is the end goal. If you are at this stage, then you are all set!

Financial freedom means that your investments generate enough income to cover the costs of maintaining those properties and cover your living expenses. All of the strategies that we mentioned above are going to help you get to this point. Once you are here, you can keep investing, or you can sit back and relax. The choice is up to you.

***

By now, we hope that you have a pretty good idea of where you are financially in this present moment and the steps that you want to take to move forward.

There is still a lot of information to cover before you can get started investing, but now is a good time to pause and create an actionable plan. Right now, it does not have to be perfect. It does not have to be full. Just start with a basic structure of the ideas that you liked. Create a list of ideas from this chapter that resonated with you and do your own research to come up with other ideas. Number this list by your interest level and start diving into the ideas that you can get started on right now.

Chapter 3: This Little Piggy Knows Which Market

Do you know the little thing that adults do to babies' toes? This little piggy went to the market, this little piggy stayed home, and so on.

Have you ever noticed that no one asks which market the little piggy goes to? Maybe that little piggy actually wants to get into real estate investing. Which market is best for a little piggy just starting out?

Never fear, this chapter will answer all of your questions about which market is best for you and your toes. We are going to focus primarily on residential options because they are the best for first-time investors. If you do some quick internet searches you will quickly see that commercial real estate is a lot trickier to deal with, it fluctuates more than residential (which means there is a higher risk), and it has its own rules that are separate from residential real estate.

As you might assume, there is a lot to consider and research when you are choosing which market to invest in. The research that you conduct is very important and can be the determining factor in whether or not your investment succeeds. As you begin to research potential markets, do not limit yourself too much. Especially in the beginning, it is important to look at a bunch of different markets to get a good feel of what is out there and to help solidify the process of research. Essentially, the more markets that you research in the beginning (even if it is just for practice), the more it will help you get into a good research routine. This then helps the process go faster and smoother in the future. Make sense?

Now, take out your paper and divide it into four sections. Those sections do not have to take up the whole page but should be at least half a page large.

- On the top left write local
- Top right write near-ish
- Bottom left write the big picture
- Bottom right write the small picture

We will cover what these mean in the next four sections. This is a very important step to focus on your path to financial freedom. Although it is critical to understand the different markets and which one will work best for you, do not spend too much time on this section. Repeat: Do not spend too much time on this section. Research, choose, and move on. Dwelling on the benefits and disadvantages of the different markets can send you into a downward spiral of indecision. Do not do this. You will thank us and yourself later.

Real estate often relies on quick decisions. Whether that is because of fluctuations in value or in availability. If you think about a market that is thriving, properties do not stay on the market for very long. In some cases, really good investment properties do not even make it on the market before they are snatched up by another investor. This business is competitive. If you are in an area that is doing really well, chances are you will be entering a fairly competitive environment. That is why it is important to start making connections as early as you can. The best way to thrive is to trust yourself and your goals and make an informed decision based on your research.

Let's jump back to Jerry. We saw in the first chapter that Jerry has some debts to take care of and he's making a plan to pick up a side hustle to take care of those debts while building a network and learning the real estate business from a hands-on approach. While he does this, he will be pocketing some extra savings in order to put together an investment plan later on.

Before he can build an investment plan, he has to start researching what markets are available to him. Jerry really is not sure which market is best for him. Should he stay local or branch out to a smaller city nearby?

Let's lay out the benefits and disadvantages of both options.

LOCAL

If you ask most real estate professionals, they will tell you that to succeed in real estate investing, you have to invest in your local market.

What exactly does that mean? Simply put, you look for investment opportunities in the area that you live in. At the fundamental level, it makes sense to invest in your local market. We will go over some specific benefits later in the chapter but for now, I think we can all agree that investing in the area that you live in gives you a slight advantage in the form of knowledge.

With that said, in many areas property prices have been steadily increasing over the past few years. You have probably seen news stories and read articles about how small cities and neighborhoods are changing because of niche interests.

In many areas lately, communities have gotten a facelift, so to speak, commercialized but niche yoga studios, restaurants, or coffee shops moving into neighborhoods. When these commercial businesses move in, it makes the residential prices skyrocket. This is usually good news for people that had property in the area before the big bang, but not so much for a beginner investor looking to break into the market.

If your local area is pre-big bang, that is a great time to do all of your research and get in on the ground floor.

But what if you live in a post-big bang community where the property prices are just too high for you to reasonably invest?

NEAR-ISH

Investing in your local market is the best way to invest, but sometimes it is just too expensive. If that is the case, then you should branch out to nearby markets. However, you still do not want to go too far. When you go too far, you lose all of the benefits that come with investing in your local market. As we will find out later in this chapter, those benefits are too lucrative to pass up on.

It is recommended that if you choose to deviate from your local market, start by going one hour away. Explore neighborhoods in this area. Check for direct lines to public transport or direct roads (highways and interstates).

If one hour is still not getting you what you want, try two. Anything beyond two is overreaching. The truth is, you should be able to find an ideal market within the one hour range. Keep in mind that at the end of the day, your investment should appeal to you and your potential renters/buyers.

BIG PICTURE

To begin the decision-making process, it is important to look at the big picture first. Although real estate investing is a tried and true way to generate wealth (we will discuss the aspects of this later), it does fluctuate just like anything else.

Real estate is deeply affected by outside forces (political, environmental, social, and economic to name a few). These forces have a significant say in property values and pricing in a specific area. Beyond that, the market is affected by demand. That is, how many houses are wanted in a specific price range at the same time and how many people are trying to buy those houses (you might have heard the terms buyer's or seller's market before, which is that demand in action). The market is also affected by what is called rarity, or if there is a limit to the supply chain. The market is affected by utility, how functional a property is (did the property pass inspection, or are there significant barriers to deal with before a sale can be made?). Finally, the market is affected by transferability, or a transactional barrier that stops a sale from happening.

There are also some economic factors that come into play, which means you should research an area before investing in it. You should be looking at the population growth within your market. Are people coming or going? What is the age range of those people? Is there a nearby college that brings a younger demographic? You should also be looking at what jobs are available in your target market. Is there a heavy influence on blue-collar jobs? Or maybe your town/city is starting to see a technology and service boom. Looking at these economic factors not only tells you about the market now but also in the near future. They will tell you if there are going to be any significant fluctuations that will make you either want to get in before there is a boom or get out before the market stalls.

SMALL PICTURE

Looking at your local or near-ish market from a small picture perspective is just as important, maybe even more important than looking at the big picture. Doing research on smaller details within your chosen market will help you make smarter decisions about prices (buying, selling, and renting), demand, and availability.

When looking at the small picture of your market, research what resources/services are available to people living in that area. If you already live in this area, chances are you are going to already have a basic knowledge that you can build upon.

Some factors to research and consider when looking at your market from a small picture point of view are:

- **Convenience** - Are there retail, groceries, and services easily accessible and available to the residents? If you are looking at a specific zip code, find out how long it would take a person to find the nearest bank, grocery store, or dog grooming service. No convenience is too small to consider. Consider them individually and together.

- **Walkability** - Track this at the same time that you track convenience. Look if there are walkable paths to certain conveniences. If there are, how are those paths maintained? Are they easily accessible to everyone in the area that you are looking at, or just a portion of the residents?

- **Public transportation** - If there is a walkability factor to your area, does that walkability lead to any form of public transport? Write down bus stops, train stops, Uber, or cab services. Keep track of those options, especially if there is no walkability to conveniences since residents are going to need an alternative.

- **Schools** - Research the nearest schools per zip code. Take a look at what their ratings are. What is the student to teacher ratio? Are the schools walkable from your preferred zip code? If you are selling or renting to families, this is going to be top of mind for them. Even if you sell or rent to singles, school ratings often influence the population demographics.

- **Crime rates** - Does your zip code have any significant crime history? If it does, what are local authorities doing to change this? How do they respond to crime? What crime prevention organizations are available to residents? Crime rates are not only important to your potential buyers or renters, but also to you. Damage to your property could cost you unnecessary expenses.

- **Neighborhoods** - Research how the neighborhoods are structured. Are they developments? Do they have any extra organizations or rules (like homeowner's associations)? Are there gated communities nearby that might change the landscape or pricing of your targeted area.

Most of these small picture considerations go hand in hand. While you are researching one, jot down things that relate to other categories. Knowing these small factors about your targeted market is going to give you a leg up on other investors. It will also help you sell a place to potential clients or renters.

BENEFITS

In the end, there are significant factors that come into play when choosing which market to invest in. Overall, the best market to start out in is your local market. If this really is not a viable option for you for whatever reason, the experts will encourage you to not stray too far.

As we talked about, the benefits of having an intimate knowledge of your local market outweigh any potential benefit of investing farther away.

When you do your research correctly, you will know what other investors are in your area. This is great not only from a competitor's standpoint but also from a networking point of view. When you know your local market, you will have a leg up on outsiders because you will know who is who (so to speak). In turn, this will help you make decisions, set goals, and seek out financing, among other things.

You will also have an intimate knowledge of the market conditions. As we mentioned in the beginning of the chapter, real estate markets fluctuate. Having an innate knowledge of your own market will help you trace those fluctuations and make smarter decisions that are going to impact your business. Is the market growing or standing still? Is it a buyer's market or a seller's market? Knowing these conditions of your own market is going to let you know if you should hold on to a property or if you will have any interested tenants for a rental until.

These are just a few examples, can you think of any others? Go ahead and jot down some benefits to knowing your own market before continuing to the next chapter.

***

Now that you know that local investments are highly recommended, check out your local area. Find some neighborhoods that you like that are up and coming. We will dive into the specific criteria that you should look at to evaluate neighborhoods in the next sections, but for now, it is important to have a few zip codes handy to use for research later.

Even if you think that your local area is too expensive to invest in, still pick out the zip code of a neighborhood that you like. Research this area with the above criteria in mind. Then pick out a few zip codes in near-ish areas and do the same research. When you have enough information, compare and contrast your findings. Jot down similarities and differences. Put together a benefits and drawbacks list, then make your decision based on your findings. An informed decision is always the best decision.

Chapter 4: Write It Up

Now that you know where you stand financially, how to take your finances to the next level, and which market is best for you. We are going to keep building on this while we talk about the next step toward investing, that is the write up.

It is great that you have all of this research about where you want to invest already done. You know what you want, now it is time to tell others what you want and how you want to get it. This part is important to organize your goals and can be used to share with potential partners, investors, and leads like real estate agents who are going to help you find the right properties that fit your criteria.

We can break this written form down into two categories, your target property and the numbers.

TARGET PROPERTY

This section of your write up will use your research from the last section. Remember the target zip-codes that you wrote down? This is where we get to use them!

In addition to your research, you will also need to pick a niche in the overall market that you are aiming to invest in. What is a market niche? A market niche is a specific subgroup of an overall market. This could be as simple as a geographic area or as specific as a certain type of property. Just like knowing your local market gives you an advantage over other investors, choosing a niche and becoming knowledgeable within that niche will give you the same advantages. When it comes to real estate, it is better to know more about a specific area versus knowing a little about a lot of areas.

When choosing your niche, you should consider a few things. First, what is available in your target market. By now, you know the general area that you want to find investment properties in. If you want to invest in single-family homes, you should make sure that the area you are looking in has lots of single-family homes available. Second, think about areas that you are interested in. Do you have a soft spot for renovating or preserving historic homes? Are you interested in more modern architecture? By choosing a niche within your own areas of interest, you are setting yourself up to really enjoy your investments.

Here are some specific examples of different niches that you might encounter in the real estate business.

PROPERTY NICHE

1. Single-family houses
2. Duplexes/triplexes/quads
3. Condos/townhouses
4. Small or large apartment buildings
5. Mobile homes on land or mobile home parks
6. Land

SELLER NICHE
1. Pre-foreclosures/short sales
2. Foreclosure auctions
3. Bank-owned properties
4. Bankruptcy
5. Burned out landlords
6. Estates/probates
7. Damaged homes (natural disasters, etc.)
8. Code violations
9. Tax delinquents

END-USER NICHE
1. Short-term rentals (Airbnb opens a new market)
2. Long-term rentals
3. Vacation rentals
4. Student rentals
5. Government assistance
6. Rent to own/seller financing

WRITE IT DOWN

Once you have your research completed and you have chosen an overall niche, it is time to then write it all down into a neat investment profile. The best part about it is that it does not have to be too complicated.

Let's bring Jerry in to write up his example profile which will give you a good idea of what yours should look like. Based on his research, Jerry knows that he wants to invest in properties in the zip code 123456. He wants to focus on his chosen niche of single-family homes. In his research, he found that houses in the 123456 zip code vary from 2-4 bedrooms and $100,000-$300,000. Based on this information, here is Jerry's write up:

Single-family houses with two bedrooms and one bath in the 123456 zip code. Target full market price range is between $115,000 and $170,000. Properties are on quiet streets near 123456 schools with quick and easy access to the local public transport hubs. Ideal properties include a backyard and carport or garage.

There you have it! Just like that, you can see how Jerry used his research to find little pockets within his target area that will work the best for him.

Although properties in the area that he is looking at have a large price range based on size and location, Jerry has chosen to look at properties at the lower end of this range.

In this example, Jerry only looked at one zip code. In a real situation, you should be looking at at least three zip codes that are closely related in market style and are geographically close. Of course, you could pick just one zip code, that just means that you have a very narrow realm to look at. By picking multiple zip codes, you give yourself more room to find the perfect investment property for you.

Of course, you should be flexible when it comes down to actually searching for properties. This write-up is just a guide in order to show potential partners and investors that you have done your research and that you know what you want. As time moves on, you can always go back and adjust your criteria as needed with no problem.

Another way to think about this write up is to think about it as an elevator pitch. When you start branching out and expanding your network and connections, people are going to ask what you are looking for and what areas you are looking in. When you have this write up already done and accessible, you can tell people with confidence what it is that you are looking for. Not only does this look impressive, but it also shows other investors and financiers that you did your research and that you are very serious about your goals. Not only will you improve your reputation within your real estate community, but you might also find leads to great properties or opportunities by talking about your goals with other people. Yes, the real estate business can be competitive. It can also be collaborative. Keep this in mind as you start to get out there.

Chapter 5: There's No 'I' in Team

We have covered some important information so far, yet nothing is quite as important as this next chapter. Next, we are going to talk about the very foundation of your future success in real estate investing. That is, your team. If you think of your investment as a child, you need a strong foundation of support and resources before you even begin. Those supports and resources are going to help you raise a healthy child. Take that metaphor and apply it to real estate to get the same idea going. If you pull together a strong team of supporters that you can turn to when you have questions or concerns, need help with a problem, or just need help pushing forward, you will have a better chance of success. No one can do this alone.

One of the most important things to focus on when starting out is how to build a strong and supportive team and network connections. This is not a business that you can go into alone. In fact, it is nearly impossible to invest in real estate alone. You need people around you to lift you up (so to speak) and experts that you can turn to for advice and guidance. Beyond that, you need to have connections to people working in the business like other investors and people offering services. We will look at the specifics in a little bit.

Take Jerry for example. Jerry wanted to get involved in real estate investing. He has always considered himself a smart and capable guy. Before he started to learn about the business, he thought he could do it all alone. In a hypothetical situation, if Jerry were to go out and try to invest on his own, without consulting anyone or networking, Jerry would not be able to do anything. That is the simple truth.

Do not be like Jerry. Be smart and put together two groups of people that will help you build your real estate business.

This is just about the only section of real estate investing that is going to look similar for everyone. Everyone that gets involved in real estate investing puts together a team of people that we are going to list below.

To make it simple for you, we are going to break up your team into two different categories. The first we will call your VIP circle, the second we will refer to as the growth team. We break up these two groups of people, primarily to differentiate them from each other. Within these two groups, you can build your own version, but chances are that they are going to look pretty similar to what we list below. Keep that in mind and let's get to building our teams.

VIP CIRCLE

This is a small, select group of people that will be involved in the most intimate decisions during this process. Secret invitations, if desired, may be used. We joke about this, but realistically you are only going to want to invite people into this circle that you can trust entirely. VIP stands for very important persons, and this is exactly who you are going to invite into this group. Only the most important people to you and your business.

As is the case with most VIP's, you shouldn't let just anyone into your circle. Family members, spouses, good friends, potential business partners, or mentors/advisers that you meet while networking. You will need to turn to these people when you get frustrated or in a bind.

When you are starting out and taking a hands-on approach to your investments, these are also going to be the people that you ask to help you. Whether it is moving furniture, painting walls, etc., asking for help in the beginning is a great way to save a little money. Just make sure that you thank people for helping; pizza is always welcome.

For example, let's say that our main man, Jerry, buys his first investment property. It is a small, single-family home that he is going to update and sell quickly in order to make a fast profit. Jerry wants to save as much money as he can during this time because he is just starting out. Jerry also does not have a bunch of trusted service connections, so he decides to do most of the updates himself (leaving only the more complicated updates, like electrical work and plumbing, to the professionals). Jerry reaches out to a few friends and family to ask them if they can help out, promising to feed them if they do. Never underestimate the power of food as persuasion. Jerry's friends and family agree to help him out, and they get most of the updates completed in a long weekend. Jerry is able to save a significant amount of money this way, which he then plans to put back into another investment opportunity.

This really is not a long-term solution. You can't rely on the good grace of people forever. Eventually, you are going to have to hire service teams to come in and do the job for you. However, when you are just starting out, do not neglect to ask for help. You will be surprised who comes to help you in your time of need.

We will discuss business partners later in the book, but if you are thinking of going in on an investment with a business partner, they are probably going to overlap with someone in this group (i.e., spouse, friend, or family). Choosing someone that is close to you to be your business partner is a good idea because your close personal relationship could lead to a very dynamic working relationship. As we will discuss later, you just have to make sure that you can communicate effectively with this person. Effective communication is the key to unlocking a successful working relationship.

SUB-CIRCLE

Within this VIP circle, you also need a small sub-circle of trusted business professionals that you can turn to. These are the people that are going to help you accomplish business-related tasks. We put them in a sub-circle of the VIP group because they also support you in very important and crucial ways. These are going to be your property manager (we will discuss whether or not to use a property manager in Chapter 7), business-specific attorney, certified public accountant, and lenders (we will discuss your different lending options in Chapter 6).

This set of people belongs in your VIP circle for a few reasons. First, once you find your person, you are going to keep using that person. For example, your business attorney. After you do your research and get referrals from other investors and mentors, you are going to pick one attorney. If you like the work that they do, you are going to keep them on as your attorney and continue to build a professional relationship with them. As long as they stay in the business, they are going to help you with every new investment property that you take on. This is a relationship that you should work hard to cultivate because you are going to rely on them for a number of different things.

GROWTH TEAM

The second group we will call your growth team. These are the people that you find through networking to help support you in smaller/more specific ways. Their small and specific contributions are going to help you grow (get it?). These people are your home inspectors, handymen, painters, landscapers, pest control, general contractors, plumbers, electricians, and closing agents. This is not a complete list, because there are just too many to list. This group of people is also going to change as you change. You might find a plumber that you trust and that charges you a fair amount for the work that needs to be done. If you are satisfied with their work, you might use them over and over again. Or maybe two people recommend an electrician to you so you hire them, but you do not think they charged you a fair rate. So the next time you have to hire an electrician, you might look for someone different. That is what is truly great about this group of people, there are a lot of people that offer a lot of services; you never have to pick just one. However, when you are starting out, it is wise to ask around and get recommendations from trusted sources/other investors or property managers that work within the business.

Even before you start investing, compile a list of services that you may need in future projects. As you make connections and network, start making a list of people and businesses that you come in contact with. Create a type of modern Rolodex that is business-specific. Whatever way you choose to organize this ever-growing list (maybe you choose an actual Rolodex) keep the list separate from your personal contacts. This is the best way to organize and keep track of your business contacts. That way, you do not mix up Jennifer G., your college roommate's ex-girlfriend with Jennifer G., your landscaper. Not only will it keep you organized, but it will also save you from weird and awkward conversations.

***

Before we move on, let's take a moment to jot down a starting team. Start with your VIP circle and make a list of people that you want to confide in. Start to talk to them about your ideas and get their advice. You may even find some connections through the people that you already know.

This also a good time to consider if you want to start this business yourself or with a business partner. Do some quick internet searches to understand what having a business partner means. Look up examples of business partner agreements. As you start to talk to the people in your life, you might just find your partner waiting in the wings.

Keep an open mind about potential business partners, as you continue learning about the industry. Keep in mind what they can bring to the table but also consider what you might be missing out on if you go for a business partner. As we mentioned, we will discuss partners later in the book, it is just a good idea to keep them in mind as you start to think about how you want to build your business.

Finally, and perhaps most importantly, start going to networking events. You can join groups and start meeting people even before you start to invest. If there are any concerns or questions that you have, this is a great way to find answers beyond research. By asking real people in the industry, you are not only getting your answers but also making connections. You will find that both pay off in the end.

Find groups in your area that real estate investors are members of. Go to those events and start introducing yourself to people. Speaking face to face with investors that are already in the market will help you find your mentors and help you find your subcircle of VIPs. You may even find opportunities to get your feet wet this way. This is a great way to find teams of flippers or rehabilitators that you can jump in and support.

Also, try to find groups or events that are targeted toward beginner investors. You will be surprised what you can find when you start to look. Speaking face to face with investors that are already in the market will help you find your mentors and help you find your subcircle of VIPs. You may even find opportunities to get your feet wet this way.

Now, let's move on and learn about your financing options.

Chapter 6: Financing

Now that we are halfway through this book, you have learned a lot of information in regard to real estate investing. In this half, we are going to focus on financing, passive income, evaluating properties, generating wealth, and your path to financial freedom.

You have come to a point in your process where you know where you are, you know what you want, and you have a growing team behind you, now how do you get started? Specifically, how do you get financing for your investments?

Securing financing is a big step toward your goals. Let's take a moment to recognize this progress. You have already come a long way on your journey, now let's get on our rocket and fly toward the top.

Unlike other investment options, in modern real estate, financing is encouraged and often the only way to get things done. We have tried to be realistic in this book to set you up for success. When you are starting out and in this market, all-cash options are not super common. The truth is, real estate prices are on the rise. We will see later on how this actually works in your benefit when you are looking to generate wealth. But when you are starting out, high real estate prices limit some of your options. If all cash options are not super common, then what do you do?

In this chapter, we have compiled a list of potential financing options available to you. This is not a complete list for a couple of reasons. One, the options available to you are ever-changing. Two, there are just too many out there to really list. Do not fret, the list that we have compiled here refers to the most commonly used financing options and will send you on a path of knowledge that you can use to guide your own research.

If you are interested in any of these options, do some quick internet searches to learn more about them and related options available to you while you read. Because these all have different terms and guidelines, we encourage you to keep your notebook handy. This is a good time to jot down notes about the financing options that seem the most viable to you. When you find one or two that interest you, pause and do some internet searches to find out more specific information about them. While you do this, find examples of where you can access these financing options.

Since we are not actually ready to invest, use these notes just to get a good idea of what is out there. You do not have to follow through on these when the time comes as you can always revise your plan. Financing is a serious consideration because the terms have a real and long-lasting impact on your future success in real estate investing.

FINANCING OPTIONS

PORTFOLIO LOANS

It is very uncommon for lenders to advertise that they offer portfolio loans. You can find these loans by either being nosey or by having the right connections. You remember in the last chapter when we discussed your teams? If you want to get a portfolio loan, you need to dip into your diverse team for referrals. Or you can be nosey and call individual lenders and ask point-blank if they offer portfolio loans. Not too terrible.

With portfolio loans, lenders set any terms that they are comfortable with instead of being forced to follow strict guidelines like other loan types. Portfolio loans are not re-sold on secondary markets to bigger banks.

What does this mean? It means that portfolio loans can be easier to snag.

FHA

FHA stands for the Federal Housing Administration. The FHA is involved in insuring mortgages held by banks all across the country. They also offer a program to help people purchase properties in areas that they intend to live in.

Technically speaking, FHA loans are not intended for investment properties. Like many good things, there is a loophole that opens up for investors. If you buy a home with up to four units and you intend to live in one of them, you can qualify for an FHA loan.

203K LOANS

203k loans are pretty similar to FHA loans. However, 203k loans give you the ability to borrow extra money to finance projects that involve rehabilitation or flipping. This extra borrowing is combined with your main loan which makes it easier to handle.

OWNER FINANCING

Owner financing is one of the rarer options, but an option none the less. You can only secure this financing if you can find a homeowner that owns their house completely. Then, they have to be willing to sell to you and provide financing.

Some benefits to this option are that you can skip expensive bank fees and make payments directly to the owner.

The downfall is there are usually higher interest rates involved in this transaction.

HARD MONEY LOANS

Hard money loans are one of the riskier options available to you. A hard money loan is lent out by a private business or private investor versus a bank. These loans are typically for short-term investments only.

Hard money loans are determined by the value of the investment property versus collateral assets. They range between six months to three years in terms and have higher interest rates between 8-15% (8 Viable Real Estate Finance Options, 2015, p. 6).

The main benefit of hard money loans is that they are processed much faster than bank loans, which means that you can turn a pretty quick profit by flipping or rehabilitating properties.

PRIVATE MONEY

Private money loans are very similar to hard money loans in that they are not lent out by a bank and they can be risky. In a private money loan transaction, the lender and borrower usually have a close or personal relationship. This can make it easier to agree to more beneficial terms for both parties involved, but also amps up the risk factor.

Because there is usually a closer relationship involved, terms can be negotiated and in turn interest rates and fees are usually lower. However, it is important to note that foreclosures can still occur in this option.

HOME EQUITY

Home equity loans can only take place if you already have equity in a piece of real estate. It is usually easier to use your existing property to take out a home equity loan than to secure a fully new loan. Home equity loans are usually actual loans or a line of credit. "Banks will usually only lend a certain percentage, around 90%, of the total value of your existing property, minus the amount you still owe" (8 Viable Real Estate Finance Options, 2015, p. 8). Often this is enough to fund a down payment on a potential investment property.

COMMERCIAL LOANS

All of the loans that we mentioned above focus primarily on residential real estate options, with a few exceptions. If you are looking to invest in commercial property, you might have to get a commercial loan. Makes sense, right?

How is a commercial loan different? Commercial loans typically have higher rates of fees and interest. They also are usually for shorter terms.

If you are considering flipping properties as an investment option, you might want to consider opening a business line of credit. This will give you more flexibility that goes hand in hand with flipping.

Unlike residential loans which are based on your income, commercial loans are determined based on the property worth. They will be evaluated based on how much the property could generate (emphasis on the could) and your own personal financial skills and history in commercial property.

***

Again, this section is just an introduction to the types of financing available to you. This is an important step to really research and take your time with because it has a direct impact on what you can do and relates to the risk involved in real estate investing. Do your research and make smart decisions to avoid unnecessary risks.

LET'S TALK ABOUT CASH

As we mentioned, investing in real estate is unique compared to other investment opportunities because it allows you to take out financing in order to invest. Basically, it is one of the only strategies that allows you to use other people's money to help you accomplish your goals. This is great because it allows just about anyone the opportunity to get into the business. You do not need to be rich in order to invest. Do some quick internet searches and you will find lots of stories of people starting with nothing and building a prospering real estate business. This is mainly why real estate investing is so attractive to so many people, but most people just like to hear the stories and not think about the actual money that does need to go into an investment.

So, although you can use financing, you should not rely on it entirely to build your business. That is, you should always have cash set aside to serve your investment strategy.

How much cash will you need and how do you go about raising it?

Realistically, the amount of cash that you need is dependent on what strategy or avenue you choose to follow. Think about Chapter 2, where we detail strategies to help you improve your financial situation. Combine this with the information from Chapter 3 in regard to prices in your target market and your property criteria from your write-up. Finally, tap into the team of experts that you gathered back in Chapter 5 to ask for professional advice. How much cash you need is ultimately dependent on what loan strategy you choose to follow.

Let's take a look at a hypothetical situation through our main character, Jerry. Let's say that Jerry is choosing to increase his savings. Jerry decides that he is going to do this by flipping a house. He finds a small fixer-upper that just needs some cosmetic improvements to increase its value. Jerry buys the property for $150,000. Jerry is able to purchase this through an FHA loan, with a required 3.5% down payment. Doing some simple math, he can see that he will need approximately $5,250 (multiply .035 by 150,000) for his down payment. That is not too bad, but there are other things to consider. For example, Jerry wants to make cosmetic improvements to the house. This means that he is going to need to put aside another $10,000-15,000. In addition to this, he needs to set aside cash for closing costs, let's say they are going to be around $3,000.

In this scenario, Jerry has a pretty low down payment. As we now know from our research, that can vary greatly. Even with a very low down payment, Jerry is still going to need to set aside approximately $23,250 to invest in this property. Now think about a scenario where you are required to put down a larger down payment. You can see from this that the cash that you need to invest in a property can be rather significant, especially if you are starting out from one of the first two financial stages. However, you have some options available to you.

Okay, so you will need some money in order to invest in a property. If you are just starting out, how or where do you find that money?

Let's look at a few easy ideas.

SAVE

This is perhaps the most obvious solution to your money troubles. It is also maybe the slowest solution. Use the tips from way back in Chapter 2 to accomplish this goal.

Here is a reminder of what those were:

- Get a raise in your current job
- Work for extra income in a side hustle or second, part-time job

- Look for ways to cut extra expenses in your budget

This may not be the flashiest example/strategy but it works. If you choose to follow this idea, be patient because it is going to take some time to pull off.

SELL

Are there any possessions that you have that you could sell or swap out for cheaper alternatives to raise the money? For example, do you have a really nice and new car? Could you sell it and buy a less expensive one? In a similar frame of thought, are there any expensive tools or toys that you have laying around (expensive lawnmower, hobby car or motorcycle that you rarely use, hobby tools, or machines like snowmobiles or ATVs, etc.). This does not have to be a permanent change. Once you are more financially stable, you can always get these things again.

Remember the goal here is to build your real estate business, generate wealth and passive income, and achieve financial freedom. Do not let little things like this get in the way of this goal. Parting might be hard at first, but think about all of the things that you can do when you have the money and resources to do those things. If you own a large house, are you willing to downsize to a smaller place? Are there little things around your house that are just collecting dust? Selling things is a safe and logical option to raise money for your goals.

BORROW

Although borrowing is an option, you need to be extremely careful and smart if you choose to do this. Again, remember that the goal is to achieve financial freedom, not build up more debt. If you use personal loans, credit cards, or lines of credit to make down payments, you have to make sure that your investment is going to generate enough to cover these costs. If it does not, then you are losing money instead of generating wealth. Make sure that you can handle extra payments and make sure you are not hypnotized by this quick and easy way to raise money.

PARTNER

We mentioned having a business partner back in Chapter 5, but we did not go into specifics about it. Really, investing with a business partner is a great way to get into real estate, and it can be a long-term thing that pays off for both of you. Let's say that you want to buy a box of cookies, but you do not have the cash to buy that box of cookies. An option is to find a friend and split the cost of the cookies with them. Of course, you are going to have to offer them half of the cookies. In reality, you both win because neither one of you had to pay full price and both of you get to eat cookies! Investing with a business partner works in this same way.

If you choose to go this route, make sure that you pick someone that you trust, someone that you can work with, and most importantly someone that you can communicate effectively with. In almost every type of relationship, failed communication leads to a failed relationship. Be upfront, right from the beginning about what you want and what you need from a business partner. Make sure you form a written agreement so that you do not run into any troubles farther down the line. You may just find out that having a business partner is exactly what you need to succeed in this business!

Chapter 7: Passive Income

Now that we understand the basic structure of real estate investing and some specific financing options, let's jump into the idea of passive income.

What exactly is passive income? In its simplest definition, passive income is just as it sounds, making money without doing labor. As we have seen in previous sections, passive income through real estate investing does not mean that you will not *ever* have to work. Building up to a state of passive income takes time and work.

When you are just starting out, you probably will not be able to generate passive income. The reality of the situation is that you are going to need to be hands-on at the start. By doing things yourself, you will save money. In the beginning, it will be easier to do things yourself because you will have fewer investments and you will want to know how to run things. Back in Chapter 2, we talked about certain strategies that will help you become educated on what it takes to run an investment. We spoke about becoming a buyer's agent or leasing agent in order to learn the business from a hands-on, risk-free approach. These strategies are a great way to get started. When you transfer what you know to your own investments, you make life easier for yourself.

When you buy your first investment property, you will put these learnings into practice, and you will want to keep them in line by doing them yourself or with your investment partner.

That is truly a smart and good way to start. But after a while, you might not want to do all of the repairs or be called every two days because a tenant has a leaky faucet. Thankfully you have options available to you. Let's take a look at the two different strategies that you can choose from. The first is called active income, and the second is called passive income.

ACTIVE INCOME

Before we jump in and learn about passive income, let's talk about the flip-side in more detail. Active income sounds just like it is. As an investor, you take an active role in managing the property (or properties) that you own. Simple.

Let's bring Jerry back for this section. In the beginning, Jerry purchased a single unit family home that he intends to rent out to a family. Great!

Now Jerry has already done his research on the local market before he bought the property. He has put together a reasonable rent that will give him a nice cash flow, and it comfortably competes with other similar properties in the area. But now that Jerry has the place, he's realizing all of the things that it takes to run a property that he did not think about too much beforehand.

The very first thing Jerry has to focus on is finding tenants. Good tenants. He realizes that he is now going to have to list the property where it will be found, show the property to prospective renters, and screen potential tenants. All of this has to happen before he gets that cash flow moving.

After he finds the perfect tenants, Jerry then thinks that everything will fall into place and be smooth-sailing from there. Jerry is not thinking correctly. In reality, he still has to build a renter's agreement, collect monthly rent, pay the bills, and take care of maintenance among other things. Jerry is going to be called at 2 a.m. when the upstairs water pipe breaks or when the tenants' two-year-old son microwaves a metal spoon. He is going to have to be available all the time to take care of things. This is fine if Jerry lives nearby. But what if Jerry could not or did not want to invest in his immediate market? What if Jerry purchased property an hour away from where he currently lives?

Jerry's not worried right now because this is his only property and the cash flow from the property gave him enough freedom to reduce his hours at work. Now he has the extra time to take care of things.

Looking ahead though, Jerry realizes that this is not a long-term solution. When he starts picking up multiple properties in the area and surrounding markets, will he still have enough time to take care of things in the way that he should? We do not want to see our hero, Jerry, become a bad landlord and ruin his reputation in his local real estate market. Is there a way that Jerry can take a back seat and not have to stress about managing his properties?

PASSIVE INCOME

If active income involves taking a hands-on approach to your investment, then you can safely assume that passive income means that you take a back seat approach to managing your investments. You do not have to be a genius to figure this out.

Depending on your goals, an active approach might work perfectly for you or it might hinder your future success in real estate.

The main thing to consider when choosing between active and passive approaches is to figure out what your desires are. Do you see your investments as a hobby? Do you enjoy doing maintenance work on the properties? Are you able to answer and deal with your tenants' issues in a quick and effortless way? Or are you going to struggle to keep up with the maintenance work on your properties? In the end, you need to decide whether or not you even want to do these things. If even the thought of taking care of things on a regular basis makes you queasy, know that you have another option.

Most people use passive income to generate retirement income faster or to pay off debts. In the end, most people are able to retire earlier than following only traditional career paths (work until you are 65, then retire with a little savings). When you have quality properties under your name that generate consistent positive cash flow, you have options available to you.

Having a passive income is the very ideal of real estate investing. Unless you get into the business because you just really like to maintain properties, a passive income is your best path to success in real estate. In Chapter 9, we will talk more specifically about generating wealth.

When you eventually retire, you then have the choice to keep your investments and continue to live as you have or sell your investments and live off of the savings you have specifically put aside. Both are great options and eventually come down to personal preference.

PROPERTY MANAGEMENT

In the next chapter, we will go over how to evaluate a property properly (say that 10 times fast) and the different options available to you. For now, since we are talking about passive income, let's go over the basics of property managers.

When you are starting out and investing locally, it is possible and perhaps economical for you to manage your own properties. As we talked about in Chapters 3 and 4, there are benefits to investing locally like having knowledge of the area and building a team of contractors/handymen that you know and trust. When you are in the local area, you can easily pop on over to an investment property to oversee issues and dispatch someone from your team to take care of whatever issue needs to be taken care of.

When our main character, Jerry, got his first investment property, he took on the property management himself. It was easy and simple for him to handle. He continued to do so as he began to expand his investments to multiple locations. As you might suspect, it soon became too much for him to handle. He could not take care of all of his properties and take care of his personal business as well.

Whether you are at this stage or if you just do not want to take care of your investment properties from the start, you have the option of hiring a property manager.

The cost of hiring a property manager will ultimately depend on your area, property type, number of properties, and services that they offer among other things. For the most part, there is an industry-standard that most property management companies adhere to. Make sure you do your research before hiring a potential manager to ensure that you are not only choosing a trustworthy service/person but also that you are getting a right and fair deal. It is very wise to vet potential property management companies. Ask around, use your ever-expanding network, and most importantly do not go with the first one you find. Just like any big purchase or service that you make or hire, shop around a little to find the best fit for you and your investment. If you can't find a good enough manager right off the bat, start by taking on the responsibility yourself while you continue to look for the right fit. It is better to do things yourself than to pick the wrong manager. Remember that your reputation means everything in this business. If your property manager mismanages your investments, this not only may cost you money right off the bat, but it may also harm your reputation in your local market. Once the word gets around, you are going to need to do significant damage control to fix it.

It may seem enticing to only consider what a property manager costs, but it is also important to consider what a property manager brings to the table. The first and most obvious benefit of hiring a property manager is that they will take care of your property for you. This means you do not have to take care of the property. Pretty straightforward, we know it sounds a little silly to write it out this way, but you might be surprised just how many headaches managers can save you.

In addition, here is a list of other benefits a property manager can bring to your investment:

- Collecting rent
- Dealing with evictions and late rents

- Knowledge of the market
- Dealing with tenants
- Screening tenants
- Paying the bills for the property
- General maintenance
- Listing rental spaces and handling showings

Do not underestimate the power of a manager's knowledge of the market. As we have said repeatedly, your connections are your power in this industry. If you team up with someone (specifically a manager in this case) that has been working in the industry for years and that has built up their own team of industry professionals, then you not only have access to these connections but you also know that your property is going to be taken care of.

These are just some simple examples of some things you might not think about when looking at your investment property, and with the help of a property manager, you won't have to! Remember that a property manager will take care of everything, and you will only have to worry about major issues that might pop up occasionally. This does not sound like too bad of a deal when you consider everything together.

As another reminder, consider what you want first. If you like to have control over your investment properties, hiring a property manager might not be right for you. If you view real estate investing as more of a hobby, hiring a property manager might not be right for you. As in everything else, making this decision needs to work for you and your potential buyers/renters. If you decided to take the active approach, do you realistically have enough time to dedicate to maintaining the property? If not, this could reflect badly on your reputation.

Go ahead and take out that piece of paper again. Make two personalized pros and cons lists. Have one focus on if you managed the property and the other if you hired a property manager. Are there any areas that overlap? Or does one approach look more favorable to you? Make a temporary decision right here and now, just know that you can always change your mind!

Chapter 8: Property Know-How

Let's take a moment to review what we have gone over so far. So far, we have learned how to take stock of our current financial state, how to move beyond your current financial state, which market is best for you, how to write up an investment profile based on your market research, why building a team is critical to your success in real estate, what financing options are available to you, and the difference between passive and active income strategies. Whew! That's a mouthful. Before we jump into the next section, let's take a moment to reflect on all that we have learned.

We are now nearing the end of this book and we hope that your imagination has been sparked. We still have a bit to get through, so let's take a deep breath together. In and out. Feel better?

Let's talk about your property. Before you decide to invest in a property, you have to know how to evaluate it properly. We have talked about how to find property by researching your market. We have also talked about how you should maintain that property (especially if it is a rental). So now, let's talk about how to determine if a property is a good investment for you.

MORTGAGE

A mortgage is a type of loan that helps you finance a piece of property. In this specific lending scenario, the lender owns your property until you pay off the loan. If you fail to make payments, the lender can (and will) take the property from you. This is known as a foreclosure.

The terms of your mortgage are determined by your credit score, debt-to-income ratio, income, and down payment. It is also important to remember that property taxes and insurance are usually added to your mortgage payment. If they are not, you have to account for them separately.

Your debt-to-income ratio compares your monthly debt payment to your monthly gross (before taxes) income in order to evaluate your ability to handle the monthly payments. To calculate this, all you have to do is divide the two numbers and multiply by 100 to get your percentage.

DOWN PAYMENT

The cost of your down payment is usually determined and agreed upon when you get financing or sign a mortgage agreement. Your down payment depends on what type of financing you choose. Back in Chapter 6, we looked at a hypothetical situation with our main character, Jerry. In that scenario, Jerry had an FHA loan and was required to put down a 3.5% down payment. This is at the very low end of down payment agreements. Typically, when you sign an agreement you will be looking at a higher percentage rate unless you qualify for a specific type of loan, like a veteran's loan which requires no down payment. If you are a veteran, you should look into this option.

RENTAL INCOME

You should have a separate category to calculate the income that you will earn from monthly rent income. You can then use this number to make sure that your monthly rental income will cover the costs of your mortgage and maintenance. This goes hand in hand with cash-flow considerations but should be considered separately in order to keep everything in mind before deciding whether or not to invest in a property. Another thing to consider in this section is what tax breaks are available to you. Do some separate research to find this out.

PRICE TO INCOME RATIO

This ratio compares the median price of households in a specific area with the median household income in that same area.

How is the household income generated? Household income is generated by combining the income of household members. Those household members must be older than 15 and do not have to be related. This ratio is used to indicate the standard of living in a particular area. This is important to know because as we saw in Chapter 3, economic indicators determine what services and commodities are available to residents in an area. This then becomes an indicator for investors to determine if they want to invest in an area.

PRICE-TO-RENT RATIO

The price-to-rent ratio is used to indicate whether a housing market is valued fairly. You can see an example of this by looking at the 2008-2009 housing crisis when the market was overvalued which led to a major crash. If the ratio is 1-15, the property is recommended to buy rather than to rent. If the ratio is between 16-20+, that means that it is recommended to rent rather than buy.

You can calculate the price to rent ratio by comparing the median home prices and median rents in a particular market. Simply divide the median house price by the median annual rent to generate a ratio. "At the peak of the U.S. market in 2006, the ratio for the U.S. was 18.46. The ratio dropped to 11.34 by the end of 2010. The long-term average (from 1989 to 2003) was 9.56" (Price to Rent Ratio, 2019 p. 5). Markets with a high price to rent ratio usually do not offer as good of an investment opportunity.

GROSS RENTAL YIELD

The gross rental yield for an individual property can be found by dividing the annual rent collected by the total property cost, then multiplying that number by 100 to get the percentage. The total property cost includes the purchase price, all closing costs, and renovation costs when applicable.

CAPITALIZATION RATE

A more valuable number than the gross rental yield is the capitalization rate. This is sometimes referred to as the cap rate or net rental yield because this number includes operating expenses for the property. You can calculate this number by starting with the annual rent and subtracting annual expenses, then dividing that number by the total property cost and multiplying the resulting number by 100 for the percentage. Total rental property expenses include repair costs, taxes, landlord insurance, vacancy costs, and agent fees.

CASH FLOW

A successful investor in a rental property has a positive cash flow. We will talk about the benefits of cash flow and how it relates to your wealth in the next chapter. For now, let's cover the basics. You generate a positive cash flow when your tenants' monthly rent payment covers the mortgage principal, interest, taxes, and insurance for a property. If your tenants' rent covers this, then you are good. If your tenants' rent exceeds this (within reason), then you are great!

No investor should purchase a rental property if the expected rent does not cover the expenses of the property in question. If that happened, you would have a negative cash flow and be losing money every month, and eventually, you will default on your loan.

In addition to having a cash flow, you should have a reserve for vacancy or unexpected costs (we will discuss this in more detail later in the chapter).

OTHER IMPORTANT THINGS TO CONSIDER

All the things that we mentioned above are very important factors to evaluate to determine if a piece of property is right for you to invest. The list above covers the biggest expenses and potential problems that you should consider before investing in a property. But there are also many smaller expenses or rules that a piece of property might have that you need to also consider. As we all know, little expenses add up over time.

UTILITIES

In a rental property, tenants usually pay for electricity. It is common for landlords to pay for everything else (trash, sewer, water, and cable). This is especially the case if it is a multi-unit building. An important thing to consider is if you buy a property with tenants already occupying the space, you will need to adhere to what the previous landlord required (i.e., if the landlord took care of all utilities, you will have to as well). When estimating the cost of utilities, be generous as it is better to overestimate than to underestimate.

HOA

HOA stands for homeowner's association, and they put forth a set of guidelines that are enforced on a property in order to keep neighborhoods looking orderly. You need to think about two things with regard to HOAs. First, the cost. What is the fee for the HOA and what does that fee cover? Yes, HOAs enforce guidelines on a property, but they also often include services like access to cable. The second thing to consider is whether or not potential buyers or renters will have an issue with HOAs. Some people are adamantly against paying an HOA fee. This may affect who is willing to buy your property if you are selling. On the renter's side of things, you can have tenants pay the HOA instead of you paying it. This can be something that you work into the renter's agreement and it could be negotiable.

PROPERTY MANAGEMENT

We talked about the benefits and disadvantages of hiring a property manager in the last chapter, but we did not discuss what they usually cost. The industry standard usually falls around 10% of collected rent.

If you think this is high, rethink through everything that a property manager is going to take off your hands. Then consider the time it would take to maintain the potential property yourself. Chances are, the price of a property manager is going to be worth it.

MAINTENANCE

At some point, things will need to be replaced. When you purchase a property, you have the choice to keep appliances or replace them all from the get-go. This can be extremely expensive, so consider the age of appliances and heating/cooling systems before you purchase a property.

Even if you replace everything for whatever reason, they are still going to break or wear down over time. Eventually, you will need to replace windows, roofing, and siding, etc. In the summer, you will need to maintain the lawn (unless you have tenants take care of that) and in the winter (if applicable) you will need to pay for snow removal.

Make sure you consider your area and the state of things before you choose to invest.

VACANCY

This one is hard to track, but it is good to assume that your property might sit vacant for a while. Although, it is possible to buy a rental property with tenants already living there. If this is the case then you do not have to worry about vacancy right now. In this same thought, you need to consider how long those renters have been there and if they plan to leave soon. Do not be lulled into a sense of security here.

If you buy a piece of property that does not have tenants or you plan to buy a house to sell it, you definitely need to consider vacancy issues before investing. You could encounter vacancy because you overestimated the demand for the area when you did your market research. Or you might not be getting enough traffic to find tenants or buyers.

If you find yourself in the first situation, you need to consider altering what you are offering for the property/rent, and you need to consider if you have enough cash available to cover expenses for a while until you find a buyer or tenants.

If you find yourself in the second situation, you need to adjust your marketing strategy. Either find more creative ways to market, or team up with a real estate agent who has a proven track record.

Vacancy is never fun to deal with, but you can combat the potential loss by being smart and planning ahead.

OTHER EXPENSES

Beyond normal maintenance, there are other expenses that occur on a more regular basis that you need to plan for before you decide to invest in a particular piece of property. These expenses vary greatly and can include anything from regular lawn maintenance, pest control, landscaping, painting, roof and gutter maintenance, or general cleaning. Like we said, these either occur regularly or occasionally. You should budget for them nonetheless.

Another option for you to consider is to make it a part of your tenant agreement that the tenants have to take care of these things. Never assume that they will.

***

This is a lot of information to consider when evaluating a piece of property. A smart thing to do is to build a blank form that you can organize all of these criteria and fill out when you approach a potential property.

You might be able to find a blank form online if you search for one, but it would be smart to create your own. That way, you can personalize it to your own criteria and add anything extra that you might need to consider. The form does not have to be pretty or fancy, this is just an idea to help you stay organized and to help you make smart decisions, which is the exact reason why you are reading this book!

Chapter 9: Wealth and Financial Freedom

You are here, on the brink of financial freedom. Over the past eight chapters, we have touched on what financial freedom means. You probably know by now that it means different things to different people. It is entirely dependent on your present financial situation.

To reiterate, by definition, financial freedom means having enough wealth or a stable passive income to take care of your living needs.

By achieving financial freedom, you might be looking to completely quit your job or at least reduce the number of hours that you work. You might be looking to set money aside for future expenses, like retirement and paying for your kids' college tuition. Maybe you want to achieve financial freedom through real estate because you have other business ideas that you want to explore and a passive income through real estate will give you a cushion in case they fail. Or you want to travel full-time or have free time to volunteer. We could keep going, the list of reasons and ideas is truly endless. Financial freedom really does mean freedom. Freedom to do as you like, freedom to pursue the things that you want to pursue. Overall, it means the freedom to do things on your own terms.

In the introduction, we touched on how this is appealing to people in this day and age. We discussed how the younger generations are starting to find creative solutions to their present money problems and future retirement goals. For a lot of people, side hustles are the way to go. They like the freedom that side hustles usually offer. The freedom is great, but you still have to work every day to achieve some form of income, and the income that you generate is not always very lucrative.

In a way, investing in real estate can be viewed as a side hustle. However, unlike other side hustles, real estate gives you even more freedom. Once you get moving in real estate, you can take a back seat and let your properties work for you while you catch up on some much-needed sleep or catch up on your favorite shows. Even if you are not actively involved in the management of your properties, you can still make money. What other side hustles offer that kind of freedom?

Not only does real estate allow you certain freedoms that other secondary incomes can't offer, but it also allows you to generate a larger income than traditional secondary incomes can. Let's take a look at how real estate investments can make you more money.

In order to achieve true financial freedom, you have to first start to generate wealth on a regular basis. Through most strategies, generating some positive income from real estate investing is relatively easy and if you do it right, you can have a positive balance within a few months of investing.

Here we will list some examples of how real estate generates wealth.

CASH FLOW

We have mentioned cash flow a few times over the last few chapters, but what is it exactly? Cash flow is the money you have left over from the rent you have collected after all expenses have been taken care of. Almost all real estate investments have common expenses like a mortgage, taxes, insurance, general upkeep or maintenance, and payment toward property management. You only have a positive cash flow if the rent that you collect each month outweighs the cost to own and operate the property. Pretty easy to understand, right?

Compared to other investment opportunities (including other real estate investment options) having a positive cash flow is the most common and stable way to generate wealth. The wise investor will do their research and buy properties that they know they can make a profit off of. When they establish a good positive cash flow, investors are usually safe from market fluctuations. More money and fewer worries doesn't sound too bad.

APPRECIATION

With that in mind, there is another way that most real estate investors generate their wealth. That is through appreciation. Before you go there, no investors do not generate wealth by standing around and 'appreciating' their properties (bad joke?).

What is appreciation? Appreciation is how the price/value of a property rises over time. Consistently throughout time, real estate prices have always gone up. It is how it has always happened and will most likely continue to happen. That is why appreciation is such a common way to generate wealth in this business.

DEPRECIATION

You might have heard of depreciation only in bad terms. In this case, depreciation does not mean that the value of a real estate investment has dropped (whew! I know you were worried for a minute there). In fact, depreciation has nothing to do with our normal understanding of the word. In this case, depreciation refers to a tax term. In essence, it describes what part of the value of a property that you can write off every year when you do your taxes. Nice! Depreciation as a tax term reduces the burden on your income (i.e., the more value a piece of property has, the more you can write off on your taxes!). I don't know about you, but that sounds like a pretty sweet deal.

It is best to discuss this aspect with your CPA (when you find them) to fully understand how this relates to you, but here are some numbers to give you a more visual idea of how this works. "Each year…you can write off 1/27.5 of the property's value against the income you've generated…for $200,000, you would divide that number by 27.5 to get $7,017" (Greene, p.9). The final number is the number that you can write off, and more often than not, this number is higher than your total cash flow for the year.

The idea behind this tax write off is that your property is going to be subject to some wear and tear over time. It works in the same sense that business owners get to write off the equipment that they purchase/use during a year. Whatever saves you money, right?

LOANS

When you start investing in real estate, most likely you will be taking out some form of financing in order to purchase your desired property. As we discussed back in Chapter 6, this is totally normal!

One of the great things about investing in real estate is the positive cash flow that we discussed earlier. Positive cash flow is good for your wallet and your loans. As you build cash flow, you can start to pay down your loans.

If you have ever had a loan, you know that at the beginning you start by paying mainly interest on the loan. For a significant time, you do not touch the principle. Why do we mention this? Well, the more positive cash flow that you have coming in, the larger the payments you can make toward your loan. Over time, these payments are going to be put toward your principal.

As time continues to pass, you start to really dig into your loan. If you think about it, you are not the one paying off your loan, your tenant(s) are. Not too bad to think about! When you pay off your loan, you start to grow your wealth; every step that you make takes you closer to financial freedom.

LEVERAGE

So far we have some great examples of how real estate can help you generate wealth. This next one is equally as fun. Leverage. In a way, we just talked about how we can use our positive cash flow to leverage the financing of your property in the last section. Another way that we can leverage your property is to use it to make more investments.

We have seen that over time, property values tend to trend upward. As the property value increases, so does your option to refinance. You can make a profit by buying a piece of property and holding on to it. As we discussed in the chapter on finances, you can use the property and borrow against it to make other investments. The longer you own the property, the more equity you can squeeze from it.

FORCED EQUITY

Forced equity is really cool when you consider it. What is it? Forced equity is when an investor forces a piece of property to become more valuable through improvements made to the property. Pretty great, right? With things like appreciation, a lot of the value is tied up in the fluctuations in the market at a given time. With forced equity, you are taking control of your investment and generating real value in real-time.

You have probably seen improvement show on T.V. where renovators take a fixer-upper type of property, put a certain amount of money into it, then sell it for a profit at an increased price. This is forced equity in action. Now, not all improvements made to a property (whether necessary or not) will improve its value. Typically, you would buy a property that needs more cosmetic upgrades to unlock its potential (upgrades like flooring, paint, adding appliances, landscaping, etc.). These cosmetic improvements are the most common form of generating wealth because they have less risk involved. You can also find a property and add more significant features like adding to the square footage or adding an extra bedroom or bathroom. These more significant improvements will cost more than a can of paint, but you are then creating a property that has more to offer than competitors in the exact same area, leading to a bigger payoff for you.

INFLATION

Here we are going to end this section by talking about inflation, sort of the underdog in wealth building. If you do not know, inflation is when the price of goods increases over a span of time. On the flip side of this, the value of our money decreases over time. Think about your parents or grandparents complaining about how a movie ticket used to cost five cents or how you could buy a candy bar for under a dollar back in the good old days. This is the type of inflation that people usually complain about and why it gets a bad reputation.

The good news for real estate investors is that properties increase in value over time thanks to inflation. In essence, the expense of owning and operating a property does not fluctuate during the time that you own it. But as the market changes and time moves on, rent and house values increase, which leaves you with a higher cash flow over your expenses.

This not only increases your cash flow, but if you go to sell a piece of property down the line, guess what? You will most likely make a profit. Inflation in real estate is almost guaranteed because there is always a need for it. Take a look at the retail industry at the moment. The need for brick and mortar stores is significantly decreasing. What once was a booming industry, is now a struggling one thanks to online shopping. Residential properties have had the opposite trend because people are always going to need a place to live. It is a necessity of life and a great reason to invest.

Combine this with all of the other reasons listed in this chapter, and you have a pretty compelling reason to invest in real estate.

All of these tips and tools are intended to get you started in real estate investing. As we mentioned before (and it is important to mention again) using these tools will not guarantee that you succeed in real estate investing. If you succeed on your first try, congrats! You deserve a gold star! The truth is that you are going to encounter some hardships and maybe even some losses along the way and that is okay! You learn by doing and trying. If you fail on your path, brush yourself off and start again. Trial and error can take you a long way!

Chapter 10: Next Steps

At long last, we have arrived at the end of our book, but not at the end of our journey. As we mentioned before, this book is just the start of your own personal journey toward your goals.

Let's take another moment to pause and soak up our journey so far. You've read a lot of information over these past nine chapters and examined a lot of aspects of your life. We hope that you have a better understanding of your current financial situation and what you need to do to get started.

Before we jump into the very last step, let's take five minutes to reflect. Actually take five minutes right now if you can. Set a timer and flip back through the book. Start at the beginning or jump back and forth between different sections that you want to review real quick.

Take these five minutes to consider what you have learned and consider what exactly it is that you want to do next. We will come back to this and get more specific when your five minutes are up.

If you finish reviewing before your five minutes is up, take the remaining time for yourself. Close your eyes and think back to the introduction where you conjured up a beautiful dream scenario. Take these few minutes to go back to that dream scenario as a reminder of where you started and where you want to go.

In this next section, we are going to talk about how you can take the information that we have given you and put it into actionable steps. This process is going to look different for everyone based on their goals. If you think about it, real estate investing is unique because you get to determine how you want to do it. There is no singular or right way to invest in real estate. Use this to your advantage and make a set of goals and a plan that works for you.

Before we talk about the next steps, go back and review the information that we have gone over together. Refresh your memory of the tips and paths that you chose for yourself over the course of this book. Based on this review, jot down a quick and non-specific plan to get from a starting point to financial freedom. If you like, use our main character, Jerry. Make this plan specific to him as a hypothetical path. We created the character Jerry in order to simplify the process and help you visualize the more complex ideas involved in real estate investing. Do this once more, on your own terms.

To succeed in this business, you need to have a balance of confidence and humility. Keep this at the top of your mind as you start this journey; have the confidence to know that you can do this and to know that you are going to need to take some risk to do it, but also have the humility to know that it is going to take some significant work and time. You never stop learning in life and in real estate.

Now that you have a strong foundation of knowledge, what are your next steps? By now you probably have a pretty good idea about what you need to accomplish, now you need to set up a structure that will help you actually accomplish these goals.

SCHEDULE

Start by scheduling your time. We can tell you tips on how to do this, but it is going to come down to what works best for you and your life. You know your schedule better than anyone else. Ask yourself, how much time can you set aside each week to learn and work on your real estate investment strategies/goals? Start by looking at your actual week and making a physical schedule to use as a guide. You can be flexible with this because, as we all know, things change in life very quickly. Be realistic, but do not stifle your ambition. The more time you spend learning now, the quicker that you can get going and start investing. Over time, you will start to spend less time and energy on projects because you will have the experience to guide you.

If you plan to invest with a business partner, set some time aside to swap information. This is a great idea so that you know where you both are starting from. This is also the perfect time to set up your expectations with your partner. Sit down and have an honest conversation about your individual goals. See where both of your goals overlap and make sure that there are not any glaring differences in goals. You do not have to agree on everything at this stage, but you should agree on the basics. If you do not, then you might need to reconsider this partnership.

Agree with your partner on a timeline. Divide the responsibilities both in physical and monetary ways. Then figure out what your control over the business is. Are you going to be equal partners? Or is one of you going to take the lead? This is important to establish a line of authority between you. If you skirt around this issue at the beginning, you are going to run into issues very quickly in your journey. Be firm about what you want. This was your idea to begin with, so do not compromise beyond what you are comfortable with.

When you have agreed on your plan, sit down together and write up a physical agreement of this spoken plan. It is crucial to have this in writing for both of you to protect your interests. Hopefully, you have a long, healthy, and prosperous partnership together. If something goes wrong or one of you goes back on your agreement, you will now have written proof of what you agreed upon in the beginning.

As far as scheduling goes, our advice is to set aside at least 10 hours per week to dedicate to your business. This is a great starting point. It gives you enough time to get your toes wet without jumping in headfirst right away. Setting aside 10 hours per week will also give you a good idea of what kind of commitment you want to make to growing your business. If you choose to take an active role in building your business, you are going to need to devote more time. 10 hours a week is also great if you want to start out by helping other investors. Remember back in Chapter 2 when we looked at different ways that you can grow your savings while learning the ropes? If you commit to helping other investors, they are probably going to ask you to commit at least 10 hours to their business. Anything less and you won't really be helping.

Once you get a feel for 10 hours and how much time/energy you can reasonably commit to growing your business, start to make gradual increases. One week, decide to bump up your time to 15 hours per week. The week after, add 20 minutes a day. You get the idea. The gradual increase will make it easier for you to adjust to your new schedule. If you are really serious about building a good and solid business, we recommend spending between 20-30 hours per week. This time works the best for you to really get some work done and grow your network. If you are still working full-time in a traditional 9-5 job, spread out the majority of the hours over your weekends. This will help you to create a better workflow and not get overwhelmed during the week.

If your goal is to eventually work fewer hours at your day job, this is a great time to also create an actionable schedule and plan to achieve this goal. Sit down and figure out where you need to be financially to do this and what your future schedule could look like. This is more of a hypothetical glance because it is in the future, but it is a good thing to plan ahead if this is your goal. When you plan ahead, you subconsciously create an idea and an ideal plan. Then you can make decisions that will move you toward this plan.

Block out specific times at first to know how your schedule is going to work the best for you. For example, you might want to work on your plans between 6-9 p.m. on weekdays after work and on Saturday or Sunday mornings. When you are starting out, specific scheduling like this ensures that you are treating this journey as a priority. When you block out specific times, you can focus on specific actions that you need to take and hold yourself accountable.

Do what works best for you! Are you a night owl? Then do research and readings at night after work or after taking care of your responsibilities. Are you a morning person? Can you schedule yourself to get up an hour earlier than you normally do and work on your plans over your morning coffee? We can't stress this enough, find what works for you. You can read a bunch of advice and follow the suggestions, but to be comfortable and productive, you are going to have to find your own way of doing things.

If you struggle with timekeeping, create a separate list or calendar and mark down when you set aside to work on your business and when you actually worked on your business. A lot of people respond to this visualization well and it helps them keep track of the actual time they are dedicating.

Before we move onto the next section, jot down a basic idea of when you want to work on your business. Start by breaking down one week to see what you like.

PRIORITIZE

Of course, it is great and smart to schedule your time, but you also need to actually do things during that time. Now, you need to focus on doing things that are going to actually move you forward toward your goal.

Some good tips are to take a big goal that you have and work backward, breaking that goal into smaller bite-sized pieces that you can physically work toward and check out. Actually write down these smaller pieces on a checklist and physically check them off when you accomplish them. Not only does this serve as a visual reminder, but you will also feel very accomplished when you look at your checklist getting smaller and smaller. Never underestimate the power of crossing things off your list!

Get creative with this stage. A popular trend right now is to create bullet journals. If you have never heard of these, do some quick searches to find out about them. Some people use these to track and organize their daily life, work toward workout goals, or even track their moods. The best part of a bullet journal is that you can make it however you want. Start by getting a notebook that is specifically dedicated to tracking your real estate business and then make the journal work for you. Add calendars, notes sections, checklists, anything that you can think of to help you organize your goals, and create an actionable plan. If you feel like it, decorate the journal or leave it plain, it is truly up to you.

If you prefer a more digital approach, use technology to your advantage. Search for apps that will let you do similar things on your phone or tablet. This is also a great way to hold yourself accountable because you can create reminders and alerts to keep yourself focused. Set your timer or alarm when you sit down to work on your plan to keep you from getting distracted and to keep you working on your goals. We really are living in the best time to get started in real estate investing because you have all of these tools and resources at your fingertips! Do not forget to use them.

Start by identifying your next projects. Is there something that you feel you need to learn before you start to invest in real estate? Write it down. Find books, lectures, or even attend a seminar in your nearest city. If there is something that you are unsure of, take your time to learn about it instead of jumping ahead. This might slow your progress at first, but your future self will thank you for the knowledge. Often, projects are going to involve multiple steps in order to accomplish them. You might have to start out by learning something new and taking some time to research before you jump into a new project. Or you may find that your project needs the opposite plan. Take your time and go back to previous steps if you need to. This is not a time to rush things. Approach each new project or goal from a fresh perspective. Chances are that you are going to accomplish different projects in a lot of different ways. That is natural; trust the process.

Then, identify what actions need to be taken in order to move forward on those goals. Although it is okay if you have to stop and go back while you are working toward your goals, try to only move forward. If you start out with this in mind, you will have a better chance of actually moving forward. Give yourself some grace, but try to be diligent.

It is crucial to plan things ahead of time, but do not forget that your end goal here is to actually create a business.

After you have planned, actually get to doing what you planned to do. It sounds kind of silly to read this, but you can easily get so bogged down in the planning stage that you can easily forget to actually do those things. This is where your schedule comes into play. Use the blocks of time that you have set aside in your weekly schedule to actually accomplish your goals.

Take your bullet journal, digital journal, or whatever you choose to use and create lists of things that you want to accomplish. Break them down into monthly, weekly, and daily goals. You can make these goals extremely specific or vague. Whatever works for you. As you go through them, physically check them off.

Finally, identify your next actions. Yes, you should do this again. This process is not linear, it is cyclical. Once you set a goal and start making progress toward that goal, a new goal is going to appear. From there, you will have to start over again and go through the same process to achieve that new goal. Keep going in this cycle and keep the structure, you will thank yourself later when all of your to-do lists are crossed off!

If you think of this process as a game that is constantly evolving, you will have a lot of fun going through the motions!

***

You have come to the end of your book journey. How are you feeling right now? We have one last section left to sum up everything you have learned and to help you take the next steps, but for now, we are finished learning new things. Can you believe how quickly this has gone?

Before we wrap things up, stop and take one last look at your notes. Write down a summary of what you have learned. Right next to what you learned, write down some things that surprised you. Finish off by reviewing the questions that you wrote down along the way. If you have any lingering questions, do some quick research right now to see if you can find the answers to those questions. When you are finished, proceed to the last section where we will end our book journey together.

Conclusion

You are sipping your favorite cocktail while digging your toes into warm white sand. If you look to your left and right, that white sand stretches beyond the horizon. There's a tropical breeze running across your skin keeping you cool as the sun rises higher and higher in the sky. At the same time, the brilliant blue ocean, see-through like glass, laps gently on the beach providing a perfect soundtrack to your day. You feel happy and full, like you could stay here forever.

You can't believe you are here, in paradise. The place so many people dream about, but here you are. You put in the time, you made your life and your finances work for you. It was not always easy but man is the payoff nice. Right now, the only thing on your mind is what science fiction paperback you should read next. The only thing scheduled for today is to reapply sunscreen in 30 minutes. Life really is a dream, when you make it one.

It is Monday morning, but no alarm woke you up today. You woke up with the sun. Then you toasted a bagel and ate a fresh bowl of fruit while that tropical breeze gently danced around you. Your morning routine feels natural these days, it feels right. Gone are the days of just going through the motions and wishing that Friday would hurry up already. You took control of your situation and made this life happen.

Whatever your future looks like, we hope that it gives you the same satisfaction that we detailed in this little scenario. Maybe you are going to buy that mountain chalet or you are packing to take that long trip around the world. No matter if your dream is big or small, by reading this book you decided that you are going to take control of your situation and make your life work for you. You decided that you are no longer going to take a back seat in your life. You should take a moment to recognize that and congratulate yourself for taking control and making an actionable plan. As we discussed before, starting is truly the hardest part when deciding how you are going to build your new life. By opening this guide, you are taking your very first steps toward your goals.

Now that we are here, at the end of this book, we hope that you have learned some things and that your imagination is running wild with ideas. We provided you with a short but comprehensive guide that is intended to get you started investing in real estate. As with everything else in life, you never stop learning. We encourage you to take the tips and information in this book and keep researching. Dig deeper into the ideas that we touched on. Start getting your hands dirty and start meeting people already in the business. As we talked about earlier, this is the best way to really get started. You can research until you are blue in the face, but you will not truly learn until you get out there and start doing it.

We would like to reiterate, if you are very unsure of exactly what you want to do or how you want to do it, try some of the tips from way back in Chapter 2 before you start to invest your own money in real estate. As you gain experience, you will gain knowledge and confidence that you can apply to different strategies.

As you probably know by now, the best part of investing in real estate is that you get to choose your own strategy. There is not just one way to do things. This may seem a little daunting to a beginner, but that is why we encourage you to go out and meet people. Relying on advice from mentors and investors that are currently working in the market is a great way to get from point a to point b.

Almost everyone that began investing in real estate started where you are now, and most people will open up to sharing their experience with you. Do not be too shy to ask! You never know what people have gone through to get to where they are now, so take advantage of this and learn from their mistakes. You are going to have plenty of time to make mistakes on your own.

From the very beginning of this book, we never tried to sugarcoat the real estate business. Yes, we have talked a lot about how great it is to generate wealth and how stable it is to achieve a passive income, but we have also focused on how difficult it can be. This industry is not for the faint of heart. If you go in and expect to be a perfect investor right away, you will probably run into some significant struggles. Go in knowing that you are going to encounter some difficulties along the way, and you will be more comfortable when it happens.

Set everything aside for a moment and look back to the beginning of your notes. Remember how we had you set your goal aside, boxed off on the corner of your paper. Take a good look at that right now. Now flip back through your notes. Have your goals changed at all during the course of this book? If they have not, do not worry, this just means that you know what you want. That is great! If they have changed, go ahead and write your altered goals down on a blank sheet of paper. Now take this piece of paper and hang it somewhere in your living quarters that you are going to see every day. Good places are on your fridge or your bathroom mirror.

Place it somewhere where you will not be able to ignore it.

We ask you to do this because when you have that constant visual reminder of your goals, you are going to consciously and subconsciously focus on them. Seeing your goals written down every day is going to remind you to carve out time, and it is going to show you just how far you have come.

Remember that it is okay to have your goals or criteria change over time. As you grow your business, new opportunities are going to arise that you might never imagine could happen. Be sure to be flexible in your journey. Yes, keep your original goals in mind as you start, but know that things could change for better or worse and you might have to adjust your end goals. Maybe your goal right now is just to focus on generating a passive income in order to pay off debts quicker. What happens when you pay off those debts? Are you just going to leave investing, or are you going to continue to grow and learn by focusing on new goals?

In the end, our goal here was to get you started by introducing you to beginner-friendly tips and tricks. We want to help you be realistic about the time and effort that goes into real estate investing. We also want to make sure that you know that there is risk involved in this business. Ultimately, we hope that you have gained a balanced idea of what you need to succeed in this business.

Okay, we have done our part, now it is time to get going on your part. Get out there, keep learning, and we will be with you every step of the way cheering you on!

This is the beginning of the rest of your life. Now hurry, your cocktail is getting warm in the sun.

References

8 Viable Real Estate Finance Options. (2015, November 30). Capital Concepts. http://www.4smartmoney.com/8-viable-real-estate-finance-options/

Assis, B. (2018). Aerial photography of rural photo. In *unsplash*. https://unsplash.com/photos/r3WAWU5Fi5Q

Baker, J. (2017). White neon light signage. In *unsplash*. https://unsplash.com/photos/3T09V42K0Ag

Brew, M. (2020). 1 U.S. dollar bill. In *unsplash*. https://unsplash.com/photos/irJMm9UXmbU

Carsons-Peters, G. (2017). Person writing bucket list on book. In *unsplash*. https://unsplash.com/photos/r3WAWU5Fi5Q

Chen, N. (2019). Red Envelope. In *unsplash*. https://unsplash.com/photos/86rFYHziFi4

Greene, D. (n.d.). *Why Real Estate Builds Wealth More Consistently Than Other Asset Classes*. Forbes. Retrieved August 14, 2020, from https://www.forbes.com/sites/davidgreene/2018/11/27/why-real-estate-builds-wealth-more-consistently-than-other-asset-classes/#1c9a98dc5405

Hargrave, M. (2019) *Price-to-Rent Ratio*. Investopedia. https://www.investopedia.com/terms/p/price-to-rent-ratio.asp

Heftiba, T. (2017). Person holding mason jar filled with juice at daytime. In *unsplash*. https://unsplash.com/photos/bvhEYmFU7ec

Heimplatz, P. (2017). Person standing on a hill. In *unsplash*. https://unsplash.com/photos/EAvS-4KnGrk

Hills, J. (2014). Person wearing green pants. In *unsplash*. https://unsplash.com/photos/bt-Sc22W-BE

Janssens, E. (2017). White ceramic mug with coffee on top of a planner. In *unsplash*. https://unsplash.com/photos/aQfhbxailCs

Perkins, P. (2020). Living Room. In unsplash. https://unsplash.com/photos/G3qlZQXsBOE

www.ingramcontent.com/pod-product-compliance
Lightning Source LLC
Chambersburg PA
CBHW050003230526
45465CB00003BB/1238